W9-BXQ-487

Contents

Introduction

God promises to strengthen our life in Christ as we study His Word. The Our Life in Christ Bible study series provides you resources to help you study God's Word. The series gives you an opportunity to study in-depth some familiar and, possibly, not- so- familiar Bible stories.

Each of the nine Bible study books has 13 sessions that are divided into four easy-to-use sections:

Focus—Section 1 of each session focuses the participants' attention on the key concept that will be discovered in the session.

Inform—Section 2 explores a portion of Scripture through the use of a brief commentary and through discussion questions that help the participants study the text.

Connect—Section 3 helps the participants apply God's Law and Gospel as revealed in the scriptural account studied to their lives.

Vision—Section 4 provides the participants with practical suggestions for taking the theme of the session out of the classroom and into their families.

Our Life in Christ is designed to assist both novice and expert Bible students in their study of Holy Scripture. It offers resources that will enable them to grow in their understanding of God's Word while strengthening their life in Christ.

As an added benefit, the sessions in the Our Life in Christ adult Bible study series follow the Scripture lessons taught in the Our Life in Christ Sunday school series. Parents will enjoy studying in-depth the Bible stories their children are studying in Sunday school. This will provide parents and children additional opportunities to

- discuss God's Word together;
- extend session applications to everyday situations;
- pray together; and
- engage in family activities that grow out of the session truths.

We pray that as you study God's Word using the Our Life in Christ Bible study series, your life in Christ may be strengthened.

OUR LIFE IN CHRIST

Adult Study Guide

Book 9

By Thomas J. Doyle

CPH®
SAINT LOUIS

Portions of the "Inform" and "Connect" sections were written by Kenneth Wagener.

This publication is available in braille and in large print for the visually impaired. Write to the Library for the Blind, 1333 S. Kirkwood Rd., St. Louis, MO 63122-7295; or call 1-800-433-3954.

Scripture taken from the HOLY BIBLE, NEW INTERNATIONAL VERSION®. NIV®. Copyright © 1973, 1978, 1984 by International Bible Society. Used by permission of Zondervan Publishing House. All rights reserved.

Collects, prayers, and hymn verses are taken from *Lutheran Worship*.

Copyright ©1999 Concordia Publishing House

3558 South Jefferson Avenue
St. Louis, MO 63118-3968
Manufactured in the United States of America

1   2   3   4   5   6   7   8   9   10   08   07   06   05   04   03   02   01   00   99

Session 1

Jesus Teaches Us to Pray

(Matthew 6:5–15)

Focus

Theme: Teach Me!

Law/Gospel Focus

Because of sin, we were separated from God—unable to come to Him, unable to call upon Him. Through His death on the cross, Jesus forgives our sin and provides us the confidence to approach God as our heavenly Father, asking that He teach us to pray.

Objectives

By the power of the Holy Spirit working through God's Word, we will

1. confess with confidence the access to the Father Jesus obtained for us on the cross;
2. affirm the Holy Spirit's power to teach us to pray;
3. summarize the content of the Lord's Prayer.

Opening Worship

Pray together the Lord's Prayer.

Our Father who art in heaven,
hallowed be Thy name,
Thy kingdom come,
Thy will be done on earth as it is in heaven.
Give us this day our daily bread;
and forgive us our trespasses as we forgive those who trespass against us;
and lead us not into temptation,
but deliver us from evil.
For Thine is the kingdom and the power and the glory forever and ever. Amen.

Introduction

"Teach me!" are words often spoken by a child to a parent.

1. In what circumstances has your child or a child you know asked you to "teach me"?

2. Why is it important for a child to have the opportunity to say "teach me"?

In today's lesson we, along with Jesus' disciples, ask Jesus to "teach me" to pray. We can confidently do so because through Jesus' blood shed on the cross, God claims us as His own dear children and invites us to come to Him at all times and in all places. God even promises that when we do not know for what to pray, He will guide us by His Spirit's power.

Inform

Read Matthew 6:5–15 and the following commentary.

About the Text

When St. Paul described the pain and trials of life in a fallen world, he expressed a profound truth: "We do not know what we ought to pray for" (Romans 8:26). How often Christians struggle with prayer! Amidst deep anguish or surrounded by comfort and prosperity, God's people search for ways to convey their fears and needs, their praise and thanks.

The disciples, too, yearned to pray rightly. "Lord, teach us to pray," they asked Jesus on one occasion (Luke 11:1). His example has instructed and inspired Christians of all generations.

Of course, prayer is not unique to Christians. Many people pray, in diverse locations around the world and with a variety of religious beliefs, practices, and motivations. But Christian prayer is, and ought to be, different from all other types of prayer. Christians pray to the true God, the Father, the Son, and the Holy Spirit, in the name of the one Lord and Savior, Jesus. God's people pray with confidence, knowing the heavenly Father hears all their requests and thanksgivings because of His love in Christ. A Christian prays, as the Spirit guides, according to God's revealed will. Where God's purpose is unknown or unclear, the believer prays humbly and in submission to Jesus' name, that is, His plan for individual faith and discipleship. Christians pray for all people, for their own physical and spiritual needs and for the needs and redemption of nonbelievers—even enemies! Jesus' followers are invited to pray everywhere, at all times, under all circumstances, and to pray together with other Christians for God's gifts of forgiveness, life, and salvation. In all their prayers, Christians enjoy one extra blessing: the Holy Spirit prays with and for God's people. "The Spirit helps us in our weaknesses ... The Spirit intercedes for the saints in accordance with God's will" (Romans 8:26–27). St. Paul's words are a source of comfort and delight for disciples.

The Lord's Prayer is the model, the standard, for His disciples. Before Jesus speaks it, though, He gives basic principles for authentic prayer. Let prayer be personal, private, and communal, but never for public display. Offer prayers sincerely, reverently, faithfully, but without pretense or senseless repetition. The Father in heaven, Jesus assures the disciples, knows, understands, and hears the prayers of His children. Prayer is simply communication within the family.

Jesus prays, then, "Our Father in heaven." "Our" reminds us that all believers are God's children and members of His family on earth. Love prompts us to offer our petitions with the petitions of many others—we live and serve *together*. By calling God "Father," we are praying in the name of His Son, Jesus, who makes us brothers and sisters—joint heirs—in one family. We stand in a special relationship, adopted by grace through faith in Christ.

The Father is "in heaven," the almighty God who reigns throughout the universe yet in mercy watches over His creation on earth.

King Solomon, in his prayer at the dedication of the temple, entreated God to "hear from heaven, Your dwelling place"

(2 Chronicles 6:21, 30, 33). Though God indeed is far above the ordinary ways and means of human life, He promises to hear and answer our prayers in His compassion and infinite power.

"Hallowed be Your name." Christians do not make God's name holy by our prayers or efforts; God *is* holy, and His name endures through all time as awesome and majestic. Many of the psalms invite God's people to call upon, to sing praise to, and to "glory in" His name. When Jesus prays, "hallowed be Your name," His words are doxology; He expresses who and what God is. But the petition also invites God's presence in His children's lives. When His Word is proclaimed and believed and lived in truth and purity, Martin Luther notes, "God's name is kept holy." Jesus here expresses positively what the commandment "You shall not misuse the name of the Lord your God" expresses negatively.

Everyone who believes in Jesus is part of God's kingdom. "Your kingdom come" is a present and future reality. The kingdom of forgiveness is here today, revealed in Jesus' life, death, and resurrection; the Good News is reaching people around the world.

God's kingdom will also grow as the Word is proclaimed to future generations. One day, too, the kingdom will be fully revealed.

"Your kingdom come" articulates the deep conviction that God will protect His people and will use us to bring the Gospel to others.

"Your will be done on earth as it is in heaven." Nothing hinders God's will in heaven, where angels and saints dwell in eternal praise and peace. But on earth God's good and gracious will is opposed by the devil, the world, and our sinful nature. As Christians seek God's kingdom, we pray that God will, by His grace and strength alone, overcome human sin and unbelief. As we hear and learn His Word, the Spirit moves our will to conform to our Savior's will.

The petition "Give us today our daily bread" best expresses our need for God's constant care for our physical wholeness. The Book of Proverbs offers a godly perspective:

> Give me neither poverty nor riches, but give me only my daily bread. Otherwise, I may have too much and disown You and say, "Who is the Lord?" Or I may become poor and steal, and so dishonor the name of my God. (Proverbs 30:8–9)

To be sure, "daily bread" includes much more than literal bread on the table. Luther's insight, "everything that has to do with the support and needs of the body," aptly captures the meaning.

But the petition also draws our attention to true priorities, that is, contentment in our earthly needs to pursue the riches of the kingdom.

"Forgive us our debts." The word *debt* encompasses all the moral liability we have before God as a result of disobedience.

Luke's account has "sins," with emphasis on actions—thoughts, words, deeds—contrary to the perfect will and Law of God.

In both instances, though, we acknowledge our guilt and responsibility before the righteous God. All human beings by nature are separated from the life of holiness and truth. We stand in dire need of full forgiveness.

"As we also have forgiven our debtors." God's forgiveness does not depend upon human forgiveness. A clear illustration of Jesus' teaching is the parable of the unmerciful servant, who refuses to forgive a minor debt, though he has been forgiven an enormous debt (Matthew 18:21–35). God's forgiveness is motivated solely by His mercy and love in Christ. He freely pardons all who trust in Jesus for salvation. No human merit or effort prompts God to love His creation. Yet a thankless heart, full of bitterness and rage toward others, does not really receive God's forgiveness.

To the contrary, an individual who willfully, persistently refuses to forgive another human being shows clear contempt for God's forgiveness. Though forgiving people is often a difficult, slow process, to completely turn one's back on another is to turn one's back on God. The Christian's earnest prayer is "forgive us, and give us strength to forgive others."

"And lead us not into temptation." God tempts no one to sin (James 1:13–14). God does, however, permit trials and tests to come our way. Satan and the world assault us in many ways. Our sinful nature also lures us to disobey God's Word, to choose our own selfish paths, and to reject the call to serve others in love. In the Lord's Prayer we pray that God will give us faith to be strong in the midst of temptation and to rely on His Word in all life's ordeals.

"But deliver us from the evil one." Satan ultimately stands behind all temptation. He seeks to destroy our faith and our assurance of salvation. St. Peter warns, "Your enemy the devil prowls around like a roaring lion looking for someone to devour" (1 Peter 5:8). Our constant prayer is for God to rescue us from our enemy's plot and make us firm in faith. In Christ, God promises to deliver us now and forever.

The oldest and most reliable manuscripts of the Greek New Testament do not include the conclusion of the Lord's Prayer. On a different occasion Jesus may have taught His disciples to close their prayers with these or similar words. "The kingdom, the power, and the glory" are appropriate themes for the Lord's Prayer and for all Christian prayer. Each word reflects a key topic in Jesus' preaching and teaching, and each echoes the praise of the heavenly host in eternity (see 1 Chronicles 29:10–11; Revelation 4:8–11; 5:9–14). Though missing from Matthew's version, as well as from Luke's, the doxology is the inspired response of God's people to His mercy and love.

Discussing the Text

1. What makes a Christian's prayer unique to all other religions' prayers?

2. What principles for authentic prayer does Jesus teach His disciples?

3. Summarize the meaning and significance of each of the following portions (petitions) of the Lord's Prayer:
- Our Father who art in heaven

- Hallowed be Thy name

- Thy kingdom come

- Thy will be done on earth as it is in heaven

- Give us this day our daily bread

- Forgive us our trespasses as we forgive those who trespass against us

- And lead us not into temptation

- But deliver us from evil

- For Thine is the kingdom and the power and the glory forever and ever. Amen.

Connect

As Christians, praying the Lord's Prayer is simply sharing our needs and desires with our merciful, faithful God. Many hurts and hollow places are found within the human heart. Many days bring a new measure of distress and pain. Prayer is simply seeking comfort and provision from our Creator and Lord. We pray as children who know and trust the Word of their loving Father.

Each petition reminds us first of our place in the universe. We are "creatures," alienated sons and daughters in search of a permanent home. By our rebellion, we have distanced ourselves from the holy God and His eternal kingdom. Our Father's perfect will is far removed from our sinful, selfish ways. We need daily sustenance, forgiveness, and protection.

Every prayer begins with a simple realization: we stand naked, with empty hands, before God. He alone can supply what we lack. In Christ, our Father hears our pleas and answers us with His good gifts and Spirit (see Luke 11:13). He loves us with true fatherly devotion, sending His own Son to die for our forgiveness and life. Because of Jesus, we have the confidence to approach the living God, assured of His mercy.

1. What significance does praying the Lord's Prayer have for you?

2. Why is it important that each petition remind us of our place in the universe—creatures, alienated from God by our sin?

3. How does Jesus assure you of the confidence you can have as you approach God in prayer?

Vision

To Do This Week

Family Connection

1. Make a special point to involve all of the members of your family in daily prayer.

2. Pray together the Lord's Prayer. After each petition, discuss what is being prayed in that petition.

3. Write together a family prayer that includes some or all of the thoughts presented by Jesus in the Lord's prayer. Pray that prayer before or after meals.

4. Remind your family members that, through faith in Christ Jesus, God invites them to approach Him at all times and in all places in prayer. List times and places where each member of the family has prayed or will pray.

Personal Reflection

1. Consider the great privilege God has provided you in inviting you to come to Him at all times and in all places in prayer.

2. Pray daily the Lord's prayer, stopping after each petition to meditate on its meaning for you and your life.

3. Make a point to set aside time each day for the study of God's Word and prayer.

Closing Worship

Pray together, once again, the Lord's Prayer, stopping briefly after each petition for participants to reflect upon its meaning.

For Next Week

Read Mark 14:3–9 and John 12:1–8 in preparation for the next session.

Mary Anoints Jesus

(Mark 14:3–9; John 12:1–8)

Focus

Theme: What Can I Give?

Law/Gospel Focus

Because of sin, we often reflect a "What can I get out of this situation?" attitude. God knew our sinful selfishness would ultimately lead to our doom. In a selfless act of love, He sent His only Son, Jesus, into this world to suffer and die for our sins. Jesus' great love for us empowers us to love others as He first loved us, leading us to ask, "What can I give to others and to Him in this situation?"

Objectives

By the power of the Holy Spirit working through God's Word, we will

1. confess our sinful selfishness that leads us to ask "What can I get?";
2. praise God for the selfless sacrifice of His own dear Son on the cross;
3. describe the significance of Mary's act of selfless love and her motivation for this act;
4. seek opportunities to demonstrate selfless love to others.

Opening Worship

Speak or sing together the following stanzas of "Let Us Ever Walk with Jesus."

Let us ever walk with Jesus,
Follow His example pure,
Through a world that would deceive us
And to sin our spirits lure.
Onward in His footsteps treading,

Pilgrims here, our home above,
Full of faith and hope and love,
Let us do our Father's bidding.
Faithful Lord, with me abide;
I shall follow where You guide.

Let us suffer here with Jesus
And with patience bear our cross.
Joy will follow all our sadness;
Where He is, there is no loss.
Though today we sow no laughter,
We shall reap celestial joy;
All discomforts that annoy
Shall give way to mirth hereafter
Jesus, here I share Your woe;
Help me there Your joy to know.

Let us gladly die with Jesus.
Since by death He conquered death,
He will free us from destruction,
Give to us immortal breath.
Let us mortify all passion
That would lead us into sin;
Then by grace we all may win
Untold fruits of His creation.
Jesus, unto You I die,
There to live with You on high.

Let us also live with Jesus.
He has risen from the dead
That to life we may awaken.
Jesus, since You are our head,
We are Your own living members;
Where You live, there we shall be
In Your presence constantly,
Living there with You forever.
Jesus, let me faithful be,
Life eternal grant to me.

Introduction

1. Describe a situation in which you or someone you know exclaimed, "What am I going to get out of this?"

2. What motivated you or the other person to speak these words?

3. Now describe a situation in which you or someone you know exclaimed, "What can I give?"

4. What motivated you or the other person to speak these words?

5. Compare and contrast the motivators that caused you or someone you know to speak the words in numbers 1 and 3.

In today's lesson, we witness Mary acting in selfless love toward Jesus. We will explore the significance of her act of love and the motivation for it.

Inform

Read Mark 14:3–9, John 12:1–8, and the following commentary.

About the Text

"She poured perfume on My body beforehand to prepare for My burial" (Mark 14:8). The last week of Jesus' public ministry revolves around His destiny in Jerusalem: death on the cross!

The story of the anointing at Bethany highlights the road to Calvary.

On Saturday evening, after sunset, immediately before Palm Sunday, Jesus dines at the home of Simon the leper (Mark 14:3). The gathering is, from all appearances, a public expression of gratitude to Jesus for His kindness to Lazarus and perhaps to the whole community. Simon, a friend of Lazarus and his sisters, may also have been healed by Jesus. Martha helps in serving the meal.

At the dinner ... Mary the sister of Lazarus and Martha honored Christ in a very special way. She had undoubtedly heard from the disciples what Jesus had told them about his impending death. With the premonition that she would not have an opportunity to show her reverence for him or to assist at his burial, she decided to show him her respect while she still had time. The perfume she used, an import from India, was very expensive, worth more than a year's wages. Mark and Matthew record that she anointed Jesus' head, and John, who has many details not given by the other Evangelists, relates that she also poured perfume on his feet and then dried them with her hair. Jesus himself (v. 8) said, "She poured perfume on my body." Mary humbled herself deeply before Christ and all those present; thus she expressed her faith. ...

Jesus defended and commended her. He said that there is a time and place for everything, also a time to help the poor. But since he would not be with them very long, this was the time for Mary to confess her faith openly. He called her action "a beautiful thing." He had read her heart and knew that she had done it, as he said, "to prepare for my burial." None of the disciples were present for his burial. There were only the two believing members of the Sanhedrin who had come out into the open, Nicodemus and Joseph of Arimathea, and a few women. No wonder Jesus said that her deed of faith and love would be remembered wherever the gospel would be preached in all the world.

Harold E. Wicke, *The People's Bible: Mark.* © 1988 Northwestern Publishing House. Used by permission. (Reprinted by CPH as *The People's Bible Commentary: Mark*, 1992, pp. 195–96.)

The accounts in Mark 14 and John 12 report the same event. Each Gospel provides specific details about the setting and the conversation between Jesus and His disciples. (Though similar in content, Luke 7:36–50 relates a different episode in Jesus' public ministry.) Mary's "anointing" Jesus at Bethany presents, then, both a portrait of discipleship and a preview of the Savior's death. The Messiah is "anointed" by the heavenly Father as His mission begins—at His Baptism—and now as His mission reaches a climax in His death and resurrection. As His Baptism launched Jesus into battle with Satan, so this anointing prepares the Lord for the final battle with, and ultimately victory over, death, the devil, and hell.

Discussing the Text

1. What was Jesus' ultimate destiny? This destiny is often referred to as the central message of the Christian church. Why is this destiny so important?

2. What motivated Mary to pour perfume on Jesus' body?

3. How did the disciples respond to Mary's act?

4. How did Jesus respond to the disciples' concerns?

5. What does Mary's anointing represent and how does this anointing prepare Jesus for His final battle and ultimate victory?

Connect

Reflect upon how Jesus' anointing at Bethany applies to you. (1) Jesus both knows and accepts the truth about His coming death. He leads the disciples from Galilee to Jerusalem with a single purpose in mind: to die for the sins of the world. The Savior praises Mary because she recognizes God's purpose in sending His Son to redeem sinful humanity. In simple faith, Mary desires to show her appreciation for the blessings to her family. She thus properly prepares the Lord for burial. But Mary also knew firsthand the authority and power of Jesus over death. Her own brother, brought from the grave to life, is proof of the Lord's divine strength. Mary's act of devotion, then, points beyond death to resurrection and life.

(2) Jesus always encourages a disciple's humble response of faith and love. He builds Mary up, though she faces the hostile comments from the other dinner guests. The demands of the Law, our sinful nature, even other people seek to tear us down. In the Gospel, however, we see God's love and approval. In Baptism, the heavenly Father claims us as His own. The Spirit continues to work through the Word, through our daily remembrance of Baptism, and through the Lord's Supper to strengthen and equip us to serve in faith and love.

1. What proof of the Lord's divine strength do you have in your life?

2. How can we, as Jesus' disciples, humbly respond to His great love for us?

3. How do the means of grace—God's Word and sacraments—continue to strengthen and equip us to serve God and others?

Vision

To Do This Week

Family Connection

1. Review the events of the account of Mary anointing Jesus with perfume. Discuss how the action of Mary was in response to Jesus' great love for her. Ask, "How can we respond with acts of love and service to God's love for us in Christ Jesus?"

2. Remind your family members that they are Jesus' disciples. Discuss the concept of discipleship. Disciples are followers. Ask, "How do we follow Jesus?"

3. Have each family share how he or she shares God's love with others. Discuss ways in which you as a family can share Jesus' love with others and, in so doing, serve Him.

Personal Reflection

1. Meditate on Jesus' greatest act of service for you—His death on the cross. Give thanks to God for loving you so much that He would send His only Son to earth to die for your sins.

2. Consider how you might better demonstrate to others the fact that you are Jesus' disciple.

3. Pray that the Holy Spirit would empower you through the means of grace to serve Jesus in what you say and what you do.

Closing Worship

Pray together the prayer for grace to use our gifts.

O Lord God Almighty, since You bless Your servants with various and unusual gifts of the Holy Spirit, grant us grace to use them always to Your honor and glory; through Jesus Christ, our Lord. Amen.

For Next Week

Read John 13:1–20 in preparation for the next session.

Jesus Washes the Disciples' Feet

(John 13:1–20)

Focus

Theme: Not Just Lip Service

Law/Gospel Focus

Because of sin, we often give lip service to our need to serve God and others. Our inability to serve others as God desires is often buried in excuses. God, in His love for us, didn't just talk about serving us, He did serve us. Jesus came to earth for one purpose—to suffer and die on the cross for our sins, including our inability to serve and our excuses for serving God and others. His love for us empowers us to serve others by our words and through our actions.

Objectives

By the power of the Holy Spirit working through God's Word, we will
1. confess our lack of desire to serve others;
2. describe how Jesus' ultimate service—His death on the cross—equips us to serve others as He modeled for us in the foot-washing of His disciples;
3. explain the significance of the foot-washing episode to the disciples and to us;
4. seek ways to serve others and in so doing proclaim Jesus' love.

Opening Worship

Speak together Simeon's Song of Praise.

Sovereign Lord, as You have promised,
You now dismiss Your servant in peace.

> For my eyes have seen Your salvation,
>   which You have prepared in the sight of all people,
> a light for revelation to the Gentiles
>   and for glory to Your people (Luke 2:29–32).

Introduction

We often give "lip service" to serving God and others. We hear ourselves and others say "I should have ..." and "I ought to ..." in response to some act of service.

1. Think back to the opportunities you have had to serve God and others. How have you at times given lip service?

2. What factors have caused you to give simple lip service to opportunities to serve God and others?

Rejoice! For Jesus Christ took your sinful lack of desire to serve and excuses for service to the cross. There He died with that sin and all others. Through His resurrection, He proclaims you have been given a new life, a life that reflects His love as you seek opportunities to serve Him and others.

Inform

Read John 13:1–20 and the commentary that follows.

About the Text

The Gospel of John divides neatly into two main sections. The first 12 chapters relate Jesus' ministry as the Son of God and Messiah, revealed, above all, in the miraculous signs. The second part, chapters 13–21, recounts the story of His humble sacrifice—death on the cross—and His exaltation in the resurrection. But His glory is seen throughout the Gospel, that is, in His life, death, and triumph over the grave. The story of Jesus washing the disciples' feet is a type of bridge from service to sacrifice to salvation. In the act of foot-washing, Jesus shows Himself the servant of all and the Lord who calls His followers to live in His example and love.

Though the foot-washing is not a "miraculous" sign in the Gospel, it is a further indication that God's kingdom is present in Jesus. The teaching and demonstration are, in one sense, a "parable in action." Jesus draws upon a common picture of humility and service to illustrate the nature of God's love toward humankind. The difference, however, is that He does not stop with words; He enacts, or exemplifies, the truth of His teaching in a public display of love. Jesus brings the Kingdom to life for the disciples.

The setting is a "large upper room" (Luke 22:12), the evening of the Passover feast. The roasted paschal lamb, the unleavened bread, bitter herbs, broth, and wine are on the table. Jesus and His disciples are ready to observe the nation's holy festival, but one task remains. As the meal is being served, Jesus pauses to share a final lesson with His friends.

The evangelist John roots the whole episode in Jesus' love for "His own," that is, all believers in the world (John 13:1). "The full extent of His love" entails all the events of the next days, including the resurrection.

Washing the feet of guests and masters was naturally a menial job in ancient society. It was also a gesture associated with hospitality and friendship. Abraham arranged for water when visited by three men, messengers from God; a servant probably washed Abraham's guests' feet in preparation for the meal (Genesis 18:3–6). Travelers might expect this type of service when staying with business partners or relatives or at village inns.

Obviously, under primitive road conditions (most local roads were dirt and stone), feet and sandals were covered with dust. Rainy weather only made matters worse. It was often necessary to wash one's feet merely to enter a house, in order to maintain a reasonable level of cleanliness.

Jesus begins His act of service by taking off His outer clothing and wrapping a towel around His waist. (The Greek word for "took off" also means "laid down," a phrase used for the laying down of Jesus' life; see John 10:11, 15, 17–18.) He pours water into a basin and begins to wash and then dry the disciples' feet. No one had volunteered to perform this service, although a regular duty of servants and attendants was to wash their masters' feet (see 1 Samuel 25:41). The Gospel of Luke reports that the same evening the disciples argued about their individual status and "greatness" (Luke 22:24). Though with Jesus for almost three years, these 12 men entirely missed the meaning and purpose of their Master's life!

Peter's refusal to allow Jesus to wash his feet is characteristic of his fiery, forceful personality. His resolve is noble but misguided. So Jesus tenderly explains His intention in washing the disciples' feet: to unite them with His mission and sacrifice. Yet Peter again misunderstands. He asks, in effect, for a full bath, to cleanse his body from head to toes (John 13:9).

Jesus, in turn, gently corrects Peter's misconception by focusing attention on the issue of service. (The language of "bathing" and "clean" suggests a baptismal context. The disciples are "clean" of sin and guilt through Baptism; as baptized believers, they are called to serve Christ and His church, symbolized in foot-washing.)

After washing the disciples' feet, Jesus dresses and returns "to His place" (literally, "reclined again"; v. 12). His words follow His actions. The full meaning is not understood until after His death and resurrection, the supreme demonstration of service, and only after the Holy Spirit descends to enlighten and empower the disciples. A partial understanding is available, though, through carefully listening to His teaching.

"Teacher" and "Lord" are names given to distinguished leaders by students and apprentices. Jesus is worthy of both titles, for He teaches by explanation *and* personal example, and He also reveals His mighty power as Lord. He is the prophet foretold by Moses (Exodus 18:15), the nation's teacher. He is, moreover, the anointed Son of God, promised in the pages of the Old Testament. These twin themes thus define the foot-washing. Jesus, the model teacher, shows Himself the servant Lord, who gives His life as an expression of love for His people.

"You also should wash one another's feet" (v. 15). The disciples' behavior—their ministry in general—is patterned after Jesus' example. Authority among Christians consists of love, humility, and service. Jesus speaks to the future leaders of His Church and offers a powerful reminder of their roles as servants. Like the beatitudes of Matthew 5, the statement "you will be blessed" (v. 17) describes the state of blessing and inward joy God gives in mercy to His people.

Immediately before Judas' betrayal, Jesus again highlights the fact that He has chosen the disciple by *His* grace. As He is sent by the Father, so the disciples are sent by the Lord. Whoever accepts the disciples, accepts Jesus. Whoever accepts Jesus, accepts the Father. Their ministry and message are one.

The story of the foot-washing makes it plain that disciples share in their Lord's humiliation. In faith, they look forward ultimately to sharing in His glory.

Discussing the Text

1. How is the foot-washing account a "parable in action"?

2. Describe the meaning of foot washing in ancient society.

3. Why does Peter refuse to have Jesus wash his feet? How does Jesus respond to Peter's misunderstanding?

4. Describe the significance of Jesus' command, "You also should wash one another's feet," for His disciples.

5. In one sentence, share the meaning of the foot-washing account.

Connect

As you reflect upon the story, focus upon the Lord's humble service to His chosen followers. (1) Jesus washes the disciples' feet to reveal Himself as the "servant Savior." His life and ministry exemplify the eternal purpose of God—to save a fallen world. All people are sinful, unclean. Like Peter, we need a complete "washing," that is, we need to be pure to stand in the presence of the righteous God. The Law discloses our failures, but the Gospel proclaims God's perfect absolution. In Christ, God sets us free from guilt and punishment. Baptized into His death and resurrection, we die to sin and arise by faith to walk in newness of life (Romans 6:4).

(2) Jesus provides a model for our motives in Christian ministry. He sets an example for His disciples and calls us to do what He has first done for us. The apostle John captures this simple truth in his letter: "We love because He first loved us" (1 John 4:19). In Jesus' name and strength, we serve the Lord and His people. His grace equips us for our different tasks. His love empowers us to love others and to share the good news of forgiveness and eternal life. He blesses anyone who learns, studies, and "puts ... into practice" (Matthew 7:24) His Word, and who receives His gifts through Baptism and the Lord's Supper.

1. Describe the significance of your Baptism.

2. What model does Jesus provide for you in the foot-washing

account? What motivates us to live out this model in our everyday lives?

3. How does the Lord continue to equip us for service to Him and others today? What does this say about the need for the study of God's Word, regular attendance in worship, and receiving the Lord's Supper?

Vision

To Do This Week

Family Connection

1. Take out a basin of water and a towel. Wash the feet of each of the members of your family. Then discuss the significance of footwashing. Ask, "How might we have opportunities to serve as footwashers to people today?"

2. Jesus speaks the words "you also should wash one another's feet" to us today. What do these words mean in the way we act and the things we do?

3. Pray that the Holy Spirit would enable you to be "foot washers" to people who do not yet know Jesus as their Lord and Savior.

4. Remind all members of the family of the great washing that took place at their Baptism. Ask, "Why is it important for us to remember our Baptism?"

Personal Reflection

1. Consider how Jesus has served you, especially through His death on the cross.

2. Thank God for the washing He provided to you through Holy Baptism.

3. Consider ways in which you might demonstrate a servant atti-

tude toward people at work and people in the neighborhood.

4. Tell a friend or loved one of how Jesus served you by dying on the cross.

Closing Worship

Sing or speak together the following stanzas of "We Give You But Your Own."

We give You but Your own
In any gifts we bring;
All that we have is Yours alone,
A trust from You, our King.

Hearts still are bruised and dead,
And homes are bare and cold,
And lambs for whom the Shepherd bled
Are straying from the fold.

To comfort and to bless,
To find a balm for woe,
To tend those lost in loneliness
Is angels' work below.

The captive to release,
The lost to God to bring,
To teach the way of life and peace,
It is a Christlike thing.

And we believe Your Word,
Though dim our faith, it's true:
What we do for Your people, Lord,
We do it all for You.

For Next Week

Read John 2:13–22 in preparation for the next session.

Session 4

Jesus Cleanses the Temple

(John 2:13–22)

Focus

Theme: Genuine Worship

Law/Gospel Focus

Because of sin, expressed in pride and greed and every act of rebellion against God, we are unable to worship God with a true heart. We even fight against His invitation to come to Him. Jesus was the sin payment for our failure and disobedience to do that which God desires and requires of us. The forgiveness Jesus earned for us on the cross motivates us to come to Him in worship, to confess our sins, to receive the assurance of His forgiveness and salvation won for us, and to respond in praise and thanksgiving for His love—genuine worship.

Objectives

By the power of the Holy Spirit working through God's Word, we will
1. describe the reason for Jesus' anger demonstrated in the cleansing of the temple;
2. explain what is meant by true or genuine worship;
3. confess our sinful inability and lack of desire to worship God;
4. rejoice in God's gracious invitation to come to Him in worship to receive the assurance of our forgiveness and salvation earned for us by His Son's death on the cross.

Opening Worship

Sing or speak together "To Your Temple, Lord, I Come."

To Your temple, Lord, I come,
For it is my worship home.
This earth has no better place,
Here I see my Savior's face.

While Your glorious praise is sung,
Touch my lips, unloose my tongue
That my joyful soul may bless
Christ the Lord, my Righteousness.

While the prayers of saints ascend,
God of love, to mine attend.
Hear me, for Your Spirit pleads;
Hear, for Jesus intercedes.

While Your ministers proclaim
Peace and pardon in Your name,
Through their voice, by faith, may I
Hear You speaking from the sky.

Introduction

Read the following from the introduction to *Lutheran Worship*.

Our Lord speaks and we listen. His Word bestows what it says. Faith that is born from what is heard acknowledges the gifts received with eager thankfulness and praise. Music is drawn into this thankfulness and praise, enlarging and elevating the adoration of our gracious giver God.

Saying back to Him what He has said to us, we repeat what is most true and sure. Most true and sure is His name, which He put upon us with the water of our Baptism. We are His. This we acknowledge at the beginning of the Divine Service. Where His name is, there is He. Before Him we acknowledge that we are sinners, and we plead for forgiveness. His forgiveness is given us, and we, freed and forgiven, acclaim Him as our great and gracious God as we apply to ourselves the words He has used to make Himself known to us.

The rhythm of our worship is from Him to us, and then from us back to Him. He gives His gifts, and together we receive and extol them. We build one another up as we speak to one another in psalms, hymns, and spiritual songs. Our Lord gives us His body to eat and His blood to drink.

Finally His blessing moves us out into our calling, where His gifts have their fruition. How best to do this we may learn from His Word and from the way His Word has prompted His worship through the centuries. We are heirs of an astonishingly rich tradition. Each generation receives from those who went before and, in making that tradition of the Divine Service its own, adds what best may serve in its own day—the living heritage and something new.

1. How is this description of worship different from what many people might believe about worship?

2. Why is it important for us to understand that when we come to worship (1) we can bring nothing to God but our sin; (2) God gives to us in worship the assurance of His forgiveness earned by Jesus on the cross; (3) and we simply respond in praise and thanksgiving to what God has given to us?

In today's lesson, we see Jesus confront people with the truth of their sin—they can do nothing to make themselves right before God by bringing sacrifices in worship to Him. Instead, in true and genuine worship, God is the Giver, who by His grace through faith forgives the sin we confess before Him and empowers us to praise and thank Him.

Inform

Read John 2:13–22 and the commentary that follows.

About the Text

What is true worship? How should sinful human beings approach the holy, exalted God?

The "cleansing" of the Jerusalem temple in John reveals a central theme in Jesus' mission: to *rebuke* unbelief and call forth faith in His sacrifice for the sins of the world. In retrospect, the disciples understand the event as both the Lord's judgment upon barren worship and His promise of forgiveness and life through His death and resurrection.

The Gospels record two separate cleansings (or "clearings") in the temple at Jerusalem. In John, the confrontation occurs near the beginning of Jesus' public ministry. In the synoptic Gospels (Matthew, Mark, and Luke), the encounter takes place on Monday of Holy Week. Each of the four accounts of Jesus' life focuses upon the most important events of His preaching, teaching, and healing. Over the course of three years, for example, Jesus undoubtedly performed similar miracles and preached similar sermons and parables. He often demonstrated His power over nature or His compassion and provision for His people (e.g., two sea miracles, two miraculous catches of fish, two feedings of the crowds). The cleansing of the temple on two different occasions is consistent with other major "pairs" in His ministry.

The separate stories, moreover, reveal significant differences in details. In John, the religious leaders ("the Jews") question Jesus about His actions and intent, but plan no retaliation. Mark and Luke in particular mention the hostility of the chief priests and teachers of the law. In response to Jesus' actions, they seek "to kill Him" (Mark 11:18), yet are unable to arrest Jesus because of His popularity with the crowd. The first temple cleansing, then, provokes a mild opposition to Jesus on the part of the religious leaders and temple officials. The second episode, after an interval of over two years, leads to a deliberate plot to kill Jesus as a "revolutionary" and false prophet.

After the wedding at Cana, where Jesus changed the water into wine (John 2:1–11), the Lord travels with His family and disciples to Capernaum. The phrase "His mother and brothers" (v. 12) indicates that Jesus' unique status was at least recognized by His family, although they likely did not fully understand His mission as Israel's Messiah and the world's Redeemer.

The setting for Jesus' visit to Jerusalem is the approaching Passover. The greatest of the three major festivals, Passover commemorated God's mighty rescue of His people from slavery in Egypt. All adult males were obligated to attend the celebration at the capital city, Jerusalem. In the past, Jesus regularly attended the

Passover festivities with His family and as a faithful Israelite (Luke 2:41–50). Here, however, He attends for the first time as the revealed Son of God, who has begun His public ministry to save the nation. He is "the lamb of God" who will offer Himself for sinful humanity.

In the weeks before and after Passover, the population of Jerusalem swelled with pilgrims and visitors. The temple officials and merchants would have been preparing for the thousands of worshipers with their sacrificial gifts. The Mosaic law required God's people to offer sacrifices: sheep, oxen, and doves (Leviticus 1:3, 10, 14). Tables and booths were set up outside the temple and in some case even within the outer courts ("the court of the Gentiles"). Money changers exchanged foreign currency for local coinage to pay the temple tax (Exodus 30:11–18). At times, the setting resembled a bazaar—a raucous market street—rather than the holy place of God. Both the religious authorities and the people seem to have forgotten God's Word and will for the temple.

Jesus' response is immediate. He fashions a whip of cords—strong, fibrous rope—to chase the sacrificial animals out of the temple precincts. He completely disrupts the "business" of selling and trading by scattering coins and overturning tables. All greed and commercial activity must stop! The Son of God has come to reveal the blatant sinfulness of the human heart. He has come to call God's people to repentance and genuine faith.

Jesus' actions and words are a powerful example for His disciples. They see in His zeal for God's house the fulfillment of the Scriptures. The Son of God—prophet, priest, and king—arrives at the temple, above all, to purify and refine worship. Jesus reveals that genuine worship is always worship "in spirit and in truth" (John 4:24).

The "Jews" (here, the religious leaders) demand from Jesus a sign to authenticate His mission. (St. Paul recognized the human yearning for miraculous signs; his preaching, nevertheless, focused upon Christ crucified; 1 Corinthians 1:22.) Though Jesus will perform many more miracles, one "sign" is paramount—His death and resurrection. His body is now the eternal temple of God (John 1:14). In His flesh, the Word of God, the fullness of God is revealed. Though in the past God dwelt with His people mediately through the temple, in Christ God is truly, completely, and bodily present in and with His creation.

Like other statements in the Gospel, Jesus' words are misunderstood. But on Good Friday and Easter the saying comes true: destroyed to death yet raised to life. Only after the resurrection could the disciples comprehend these remarkable promises of their Master.

Discussing the Text

1. What central theme in Jesus' mission is revealed in the "cleansing" of the Jerusalem temple?

2. What differences in details to the cleansing of the temple do the Gospel accounts provide?

3. What is the setting for Jesus' visit to Jerusalem?

4. What caused the temple in Jerusalem to resemble a bazaar rather than the holy place of God?

5. What example do Jesus' words and actions in the temple demonstrate for His disciples?

Connect

As you reflect upon the meaning of the temple cleansing, focus upon these themes: (1) God demands pure, sincere worship from His creatures. He reveals His will in the Law, most concisely in the first table of the Ten Commandments (Exodus 20:3–8; see also Deuteronomy 6:13). Yet no one measures up to these standards. Because of sin, expressed in pride and greed and every act of rebellion against God, we are unable to worship God with a true heart. By nature, we even fight against His kind invitation to praise our Maker. The Gospel announces that Jesus is the sin payment for our disobedience and failure. His sacrifice brings full forgiveness, pardon for our selfish neglect of God's Word and our indifference toward His daily mercy.

(2) Rooted in human nature is the demand for signs. We insist upon proof of God's power, goodness, and love. Sinful human beings place the Creator "on trial," when in truth we are the offenders.

We have broken trust with God by our sin and have pursued our own paths. Jesus' death and resurrection, though, are the ultimate proof of God's love. In the giving of His Son for the sins of the world, the Father assures us of His eternal care—full salvation. No greater love, no greater demonstration of His mercy, is possible.

(3) The temple cleansing is a reminder of our inclination to put our faith in human achievement—buildings, monuments, institutions. Only God's love in Christ, revealed in His Word, is eternal. All earthly things will pass away, but the promise of forgiveness and salvation shall stand forever.

1. What keeps us from worshiping God with a true heart? What enables us to worship God with a true heart?

2. What proof does Scripture reveal to us about God's love for us?

3. In what ways do we at times put our faith in human achievement? How does the temple cleansing remind us that only God's love in Christ is eternal and, ultimately, is the only thing that will provide eternal security?

Vision

To Do This Week

Family Connection

1. Write the word *worship* on a sheet of paper. Then ask each member of the family to tell you what worship means to her or him. Write family members' responses on the sheet of paper.

2. Share with your family the meaning of worship as described in the introduction to *Lutheran Worship*.

3. Worship together regularly as a family. Communicate the importance of worship to each member of your family.

4. Say, "The family that prays together stays together." Ask, "How is this statement true?" Allow time for each family member to respond, then pray together.

Personal Reflection

1. Meditate on the meaning of "true" worship.

2. Reread the introduction to worship found at the beginning of this lesson. Consider the great gifts that God provides to you through His Word.

3. Pray that God would enable you by His Spirit's power to worship Him in truth and purity.

4. Seek an opportunity to tell someone this week of the importance of worship in your life.

Closing Worship

Speak together the final stanza of "To Your Temple, Lord, I Come."

> From Your house when I return,
> May my heart within me burn,
> And at evening let me say,
> "I have walked with God today."

For Next Week

Read John 3:1–21 in preparation for the next session.

Session 5

Jesus Talks with Nicodemus

(John 3:1–21)

Focus

Theme: Birth—Death—Rebirth—Life

Law/Gospel Focus

We were born into this world spiritually dead—slaves to our passions and powerless to free ourselves. In Christ, God's people pass from death to life. Through water and the Word in Holy Baptism, the Holy Spirit gives us a rebirth to live as forgiven, renewed children of God who hold firmly to the promise of eternal life.

Objectives

By the power of the Holy Spirit working through God's Word, we will

1. summarize Jesus' response to Nicodemus' question concerning birth and rebirth;
2. confess our spiritually dead state prior to the work of the Holy Spirit and rejoice in the new life granted to us by God's grace through faith in Jesus;
3. celebrate the rebirth the Holy Spirit provided to us at our Baptism.

Opening Worship

Read aloud the following portion of the baptismal liturgy found in *Lutheran Worship* (p. 199).

Leader: Our Lord commanded Baptism, saying to His disciples in the last chapter of Matthew:

Participants: "All authority in heaven and on earth has been given to Me. Therefore go and make disciples of all nations, baptizing them in the name of the Father and of the

Son and of the Holy Spirit and teaching them to obey everything I have commanded you. And surely I will be with you
always, to the very end of the age."

Leader: The holy apostles of the Lord have written:

Participants: "The promise is for you and your children,"
and "Baptism now saves you."

Leader: We also learn from the Word of God that

Participants: we all are conceived and born sinful and so
are in need of forgiveness. We would be lost forever unless
delivered from sin, death, and everlasting condemnation.
But the Father of all mercy and grace has sent His Son Jesus
Christ, who atoned for the sin of the whole world that whoever believes in Him shall not perish but have eternal life.

Introduction

Significant events occur throughout a person's life.

1. List the most significant events that have occurred in your
life.

2. What makes these events so significant?

3. Now consider significant events in your life that have affect-
ed your spiritual life. List them.

4. What makes these events so significant?

In today's lesson, Jesus teaches a Pharisee named Nicodemus
about birth, death, rebirth, and life. Ultimately, a proper under-

standing of these major events is a matter of life and death for Nicodemus and for us.

Inform

Read John 3:1–21 and the commentary that follows.

About the Text

The story of Nicodemus and Jesus addresses a pivotal question in the unfolding of God's salvation: How does a believer *believe*? The answer is simple: Faith is a gift of God, worked by the Spirit through water and Word. The focus of Christian faith is always and exclusively the sacrifice of God's Son on the cross for the life of the world.

Nicodemus is a distinguished man. A Pharisee by persuasion, he is a prominent leader in his community, likely a member of the "ruling council" or Sanhedrin. The council was the supreme Jewish court, based in Jerusalem, and it consisted of priests, teachers of the law (professional scribes), and elders of the aristocracy. Most villages in Judea and throughout ancient Palestine had councils—assemblies to deliberate and, when necessary, to make judgments about vital religious and legal issues. Yet the Jerusalem council, perhaps with as many as 70 members, was the final court in Israel. Presided over by the high priest, the council rendered decisions on the most difficult and sensitive cases and acted as the official liaison to the local Roman administration.

Nicodemus probably first learned of Jesus' ministry and miracles through reports to the council. Later, perhaps, he would have heard Jesus preach and teach in person. By approaching Jesus "at night" (v. 2), Nicodemus shows both respect and reserve toward Israel's new Teacher. He does not interrupt Jesus' daily routines, but at the same time is concerned not to associate too closely with the popular movement. Like other descriptions in the Gospel, however, "at night" suggests a more profound significance to the meeting. Nicodemus comes to Jesus in "spiritual blindness." He lives in the darkness of sin and unbelief because He does not yet know or understand God's full and glorious revelation in His Son. The setting, then, has both a literal and symbolic meaning in John's story of Jesus. Night, darkness, and physical blindness all portray a deeper reality—human lostness—that only the Messiah *overcomes* (see John 11:10; 9:1–41; 12:35–36).

But Nicodemus genuinely yearns for spiritual insight. He recognizes Jesus as "Rabbi," a teacher sent by God to instruct God's people. For Nicodemus, though, the focus is on the *message* rather than the *Messenger*. He is able to see Jesus as an interpreter of the Scriptures but not as the fulfillment of God's ancient promises. Together with the other religious leaders, Nicodemus understands the Law as the highest revelation of God's purpose for His people. Jesus, however, is the final disclosure of the Father's will for all creation: "grace and truth came through Jesus Christ" (John 1:17). No human ability, no human effort can grasp this insight; it is a gift from God alone.

Jesus breaks in at the critical moment. The discussion will center on the Good News, not the Law. The kingdom of God is a pure gift, "seen" through the prism of the new birth. Jesus extends the vision metaphor by linking spiritual insight to being "born from above" (v. 7). (This alternative translation, referenced in the NIV note, more accurately describes the contrast between natural [first] birth and supernatural [second] birth; another suitable translation is "born anew.") Because he lives in "darkness," Nicodemus misunderstands the meaning; his frame of reference is earthly, rooted in the natural order of human life.

In truth, unless God brings about a change in the heart of unbelievers, they cannot "see" or "enter" the kingdom of forgiveness and life. Both images mean "to experience, to encounter, to participate in." Salvation comes *to* all people *from* God *through* His Son; the chosen means to effect the new birth are "water" and "Spirit" (v. 5).

"Flesh gives birth to flesh" (v. 6) refers again to the basic principle of life: like begets like. To be born in a natural, physical way is to be born of fallen, sinful parents. The consequences are obvious—all people are born sinful. "Spirit gives birth to spirit" (v. 6) is the principle of supernatural life—a rebirth from above (see John 1:13). The analogy of the wind for the mystery of the Spirit's working is appropriate. Just as wind is "invisible," except in its movement, for example, in the blowing of branches and leaves, so the Spirit is not discernible to "fleshly eyes" except after His movement in the hearts and minds of individuals.

Jesus' words puzzle Nicodemus. In truth, the Pharisee's knowledge of the Old Testament should have provided the necessary insight into God's plan. "We speak" (v. 11) may refer to Jesus' witness alone (the "plural of majesty") or to the collective testimony of Jesus, His disciples, and John the Baptizer. John pointed to "the Lamb of God who takes away the sin of the world" (John 1:29). Nicodemus likely heard the prophet's preaching at the Jordan or at least heard reports about it (1:24–25).

"Earthly things ... heavenly things" (v. 12): The contrast relates, above all, to the nature of the kingdom of God. Birth, wind, sound are among the everyday realities that offer a picture of spiritual truths. But only the Son of Man, who "came from heaven" (v. 13), has direct experience of the heavenly reality.

"Moses lifted up the snake" (v. 14). In Numbers 21:4–9, God sends serpents to punish His people for their unbelief and disobedience. Through Moses' intercession, God gave the nation a sign— the bronze serpent on the pole. Those who were bitten and looked upon the symbol were saved, that is, healed. Now, Jesus' "lifting up" is the sign, the demonstration, of God's full salvation. The crucifixion is divine love in action toward a hostile, darkened world. God's intention is that all people be saved. He sent His Son, therefore, to give eternal life. The threat of condemnation is passed for all who believe in—trust, rely upon—Christ (1 John 4:9).

Discussing the Text

1. What question in the unfolding of salvation does the story of Nicodemus and Jesus address? Why is this question of so much importance?

2. Why does Nicodemus come to Jesus at night? What makes "at night" profoundly significant to the meeting?

3. How does Jesus respond to Nicodemus' question? Why does Nicodemus misunderstand Jesus' response?

4. How does Jesus' response attack the heart of the Pharisees' understanding about their need for fulfilling God's Law?

5. How did Jesus fulfill all that God required of us in His Law? What does this say about our need to fulfill God's Law in order to receive salvation?

Connect

As you discuss the lesson, consider these insights: (1) All people are, by nature, blind to God's will. Like Nicodemus, we live and move in the darkness of separation from God's eternal light. Sin has shut our eyes to God's truth. Hostility, lust, and unbelief have plunged us into the dusky night of alienation and despair. In many portions of Scripture, God's righteous Law reveals our spiritual blindness—blindness that leads to ruin. Jesus, however, is the light. This simple promise extends to every facet of God's grace. Jesus brings us into the light through His forgiveness. He enables us to walk in the light through His divine strength. He leads us safely to the light, the joy and glory of heaven, through His love and faith-nurturing Word. Jesus calls us to see the light of His salvation.

(2) We are spiritually dead too. The Law discloses that all people are "dead in ... transgressions and sins" (Ephesians 2:1). We

live in the flesh, that is, in weakness and captivity. We are slaves to our passions; we are powerless to free ourselves. Yet Jesus brings life to the world. In Christ, God's people pass from death to abundant life. We are reborn through water and the Spirit, born anew in Baptism to live as forgiven, renewed children of God. The new birth comes to us as a gift, Jesus says. In Jesus' death and resurrection, all people witness the depth of God's love for the world. As the Spirit works to create faith in our hearts and minds, we receive His gift and hold firmly to the promise of eternal life.

1. Describe your life of faith using the terms "blindness" and "light."

2. How are your good works necessary—but unnecessary—to receive salvation?

3. How do the words *life, death, rebirth, life* describe your spiritual condition?

Vision

To Do This Week

Family Connection

1. Review the events of the story of Nicodemus and Jesus. Discuss the symbolism Jesus uses to describe for Nicodemus what he must do to receive salvation.

2. Write the following words on a sheet of paper: *life, death, rebirth, life.* Then explain how we were all born, but because of sin we were spiritually dead—separated from God. God, in His love for us, gave us a rebirth by the power of the Holy Spirit in our Baptism. That rebirth gives us the assurance of eternal life.

3. Have each member of your family create a sign to describe the significance of her or his Baptism. Label the signs "I was reborn by God through Holy Baptism."

4. Celebrate baptismal birthdays.

Personal Reflection

1. Reflect upon the rebirth you received from God when you were baptized.

2. Pray that the Holy Spirit would enable you to share the joy you have because of the eternal life Jesus earned for you on the cross.

3. Read Dr. Martin Luther's explanation of Holy Baptism in his Small Catechism.

Closing Worship

Pray together the following prayer adapted from the Baptism liturgy found in *Lutheran Worship* (p. 203).

Almighty and most merciful God and Father, we thank and praise You that You graciously preserve and enlarge Your family and have granted us the new birth in Holy Baptism and made us members of Your Son, our Lord Jesus Christ, and heirs of Your heavenly kingdom. We humbly beseech You that, as we have become Your children, You would keep us in our baptismal grace that according to all Your good pleasure we may faithfully grow to lead a godly life to the praise and honor of Your holy name and finally with all Your saints obtain the promised inheritance in heaven; through Jesus Christ, our Lord. Amen.

For Next Week

Read Mark 15:1–20 in preparation for the next session.

Session 6

Pilate Condemns Jesus

(Mark 15:1–20 and parallels)

Focus

Theme: Who's in Control?

Law/Gospel Focus

We have sinned against *all* of God's commands, even when we have only stumbled at one command. Our inability to do that which God commands indicates that, left to our own control, we would face eternal separation from God. But God, knowing our lack of control, sent Jesus into this world who, on our behalf, quietly submitted to God's will, patiently endured abuse of sinful people, and willingly sacrificed Himself on the cross for our forgiveness. Through faith strengthened by the Holy Spirit working through God's Word and Jesus' body and blood in the Lord's Supper, we are assured that God is in control of our lives—both here on earth and into eternity.

Objectives

By the power of the Holy Spirit working through God's Word, we will
1. summarize the events of the trials before Pilate and Herod;
2. describe how God remained in control of the events leading up to the crucifixion, even as humans believed they were in control;
3. confess God's control in our lives.

Opening Worship

Read Isaiah 53:3–12 as an introduction to the Passion events. Consider the fact that Isaiah had prophesied years before Jesus' birth the tragic events that would occur in order for God to provide forgiveness to sinful people.

Introduction

Most people feel the need to control the events in their lives, the events in other people's lives, their destiny. Ultimately, no person is able to take full control of her or his life.

1. Give evidence from your life that you are not in complete control.

2. What life factors can hamper your plans?

3. How can the assurance that God is in control of your life give you peace and joy even when things don't go as you plan?

As we consider the events of today's lesson, we might conclude that God had lost control of the situation. His own Son was unjustly tried, falsely accused, beaten, humiliated, sentenced to death. But God remained in control. His plan for the salvation of the world would unfold as promised—a perfect Lamb would be slaughtered to atone for the sins of the world.

Inform

Read Mark 15:1–20 and the following commentary.

About the Text

Jesus stood silently in the great hall. Hours before, He had been arrested in Gethsemane and taken to a hearing before the Sanhedrin. The religious leaders had brought many allegations against Him, but the charges were false and contradictory. (Even the witnesses could not agree on "the facts.") A final question from the high priest determined the verdict: "Are You the Christ, the Son of the Blessed One?" Jesus answered, "I am" (Mark 14:61–62).

The sentence was death. Yet the Sanhedrin lacked the authority to carry out the decision. Jesus, therefore, was shuttled off to Pontius Pilate, the Roman prefect (or governor), for yet another trial.

A Roman official like Pilate had primary jurisdiction over affairs of the province, including to a certain extent local policy and procedures. Pilate had authority to confirm the charges against Jesus; he also had authority to dismiss any and all charges and to reduce sentences. Without a doubt, the members of the Sanhedrin felt that Pilate would render the only appropriate judgment: guilty!

Yet Pilate had previously displayed a deep disdain toward Jewish religion and issues. Some nonbiblical writers described his administration of the region as harsh, often insensitive to local customs and attitudes. To bring Jesus for trial before the Roman prefect was to risk an abrupt dismissal of charges or perhaps even more serious repercussions.

Pilate examines Jesus in the Praetorium, the official guest residence of the Roman governor in Jerusalem. Like the high priest, Pilate asks one decisive question: "Are You the king of the Jews?" (v. 2). (The account in John 18:29–38 includes a brief, secondary exchange between Pilate and Jesus; the focus is on the nature of Jesus' kingship—"not of this world.")

Jesus' response is a qualified "yes." He is truly the promised "king of the Jews," but not as Pilate (or the religious leaders or crowds) understands the title. His mission is ultimately not rooted in the political, social, and economic issues of the day. Rather He is the Savior, who offers His life as a "ransom" for the sins of the world (Mark 10:45).

On the basis of the evidence alone, Pilate is convinced of two realities: (1) that Jesus is not guilty of treason against the Roman emperor; (2) that the chief priests seek Jesus' death out of envy (Mark 15:10). He therefore attempts to remove himself from the case. First, he sends Jesus to a different judge, King Herod. Second, he offers a Passover amnesty to a criminal, Jesus or Barabbas. Third, he washes his hands in mock indignation, declaring his innocence and laying blame upon the crowd.

Jesus before Herod (Luke 23:6–12). Herod Antipas, a son of Herod the Great, was ruler over Galilee and a portion of the territory east of the Jordan River. (The title "king" was honorific; Herod's actual designation was "tetrarch"; see Luke 3:1.) Though a shrewd politician and generous patron of building projects, Herod Antipas demonstrated little moral integrity in his life and administration. He married the wife of his half-brother Philip; he ordered the execution of John the Baptizer; he threatened Jesus' life on one occasion (Luke 13:31). When Jesus is brought to him, Herod is "greatly pleased, because for a long time he was wanting to see Him" (Luke 23:8). Herod questions, mocks, and reviles Jesus. But the Lord's silence is judgment against Herod. The Baptizer's stern rebuke rings out amidst the jeers and abuse. Herod shamelessly dresses Jesus in an elegant purple robe—a symbol of royalty—and returns Him to Pilate.

Amnesty at the Passover Feast (Mark 15:6–14). In some ancient cultures, public festivals included an act of clemency or amnesty toward condemned persons. Pilate uses the custom as a political expedient: let the crowd choose, then deny his own responsibility. The other prisoner is Barabbas, a notorious murderer and rebel. He likely belonged to, perhaps even led, a nationalist movement to liberate Israel from Roman rule. Yet Barabbas is the crowd's choice for amnesty; the religious leaders incite the mob to demand the release of the guilty and the condemnation of the guiltless. (All these events, though, take place according to "God's set purpose and foreknowledge" [Acts 2:23].)

Pilate's Declaration of Innocence (Matthew 27:24–25). Pilate knows Jesus poses no threat to the empire or to public order. His wife, too, recognizes Jesus as an "innocent man" (Matthew 27:19), innocent of all charges. (Her dream, somewhat mysteriously, reveals the truth; but events unfold by the plan and purpose of God.) The crowd, however, presses for Jesus' crucifixion. Pilate faces his dilemma: render justice or satisfy the crowd. The prefect chooses the easy route; he calls for a basin of water, washes his hands, declares his innocence, and sentences Jesus to be flogged, then led to His death.

Roman scourging was a terrifying punishment. The victim was stripped, bound to a post or thrown on the ground, and beaten by guards. The whip was thick leather strips, knotted at the ends;

pieces of bone or lead were often embedded in the thongs.

Pilate's soldiers had accompanied the prefect to Jerusalem to keep order during the Passover celebration. The "whole company" (v. 27) consisted of about 600 men. After stripping Jesus of His clothes, they make Him wear a "scarlet robe" (v. 28), probably a soldier's scarlet cloak, in imitation of a king's robe. The "crown of thorns" (v. 29) is a crass parody of the royal symbol, as is the staff, a mock scepter. The common greeting among soldiers was "Hail, Caesar!" The taunt here is "Hail, king of the Jews." Through each stage of the abuse, though, Jesus remains silent, submissive to His Father's will. Struck, spit upon, insulted beyond human comprehension, the Son of God goes willingly to the cross and death.

Discussing the Text

1. Why did the religious leaders take Jesus to Pilate?

2. Jesus' response to Pilate's question "Are You the king of the Jews?" was misunderstood. Describe Jesus' kingship.

3. On the basis of the evidence, of what two realities is Pilate convinced? Because of these realities, what does Pilate do?

4. Why does Pilate use the amnesty custom?

5. How does Pilate ultimately answer the question "Should I render justice or satisfy the crowd?"

6. Describe the scourging of Jesus. What made scourging such a terrifying punishment?

7. After reviewing the events of the trial before Pilate, what might we conclude if considering the question "Who's in control?" Why?

Connect

As you consider the Lord's trial before Pilate, think about these applications: (1) The power of sin is obvious in the jealousy and hatred of the religious leaders and the crowds. God's Law shows the wickedness of their hearts: "You shall not murder" (Exodus 20:13). But human hearts today are no different. We, too, are convicted by our attitudes and actions as "guilty" before the heavenly Judge. We have sinned against all of God's commands, even when we have only stumbled, and usually fallen flat on our faces, at one commandment. Jesus' death takes away *all* sin. He quietly submits to His Father's will. He patiently endures the insults and abuse of sinful human beings. He willingly sacrifices His body and His blood on the cross—all for our forgiveness. The Lord accepts His own condemnation at the hands of a Roman governor to save His people from judgment.

(2) Our guilt before God is real. Like Barabbas, we are condemned criminals apart from God's mercy. We have no hope of amnesty, for we have sinned, and sinned deliberately, against the

Sovereign of the universe. Barabbas represents every person, for "all have turned away, they have together become worthless" (Romans 3:12). Jesus trades His innocence for our guilt. The sinless Son of God stands before Pilate ready to walk the final distance to the Place of the Skull, where He takes upon Himself the sins of all people. It's the great exchange: Barabbas the murderer goes free, while Jesus the Savior gives His life as the ransom. Our life in His death!

1. We may be inclined to review the events of the trial with disgust. But if we are truthful, we must admit that our sins led Jesus on this path. How does acknowledgment of this fact affect the way we view the passion?

2. How does God demonstrate control in the events leading up to the crucifixion of His only Son?

3. Describe the great exchange that took place between Barabbas and Jesus. How does Barabbas represent every person? How did we receive a great exchange through the death of Jesus?

Vision

To Do This Week

Family Connection

1. Review the events of the Passion. You may want to keep a written log of the events that took place.

2. Ask, "Who was in control of the events surrounding Jesus' passion?" Remind family members that it may seem that people

were in control, but God was in control. He allowed His only Son to suffer at the hands of wicked people in order to earn for us salvation. What great love God has for people!

3. Share with a friend or a loved one the control God demonstrates in your life.

Personal Reflection

1. Meditate on the events of the Passion. Consider God's great love for you as He willingly offered His only Son as the sacrifice for your sins.

2. Describe the meaning of the Passion for you and your life. Write reflections you may have as you consider Jesus' trial, scourging, and crucifixion.

3. Consider ways in which you might tell others of God's great love for them. Focus on the events of the Passion.

Closing Worship

Read responsively Isaiah 40:28–31.

Leader: Do you not know? Have you not heard?

Participants: The LORD is the everlasting God, the Creator of the ends of the earth.

Leader: He will not grow tired or weary, and His understanding no one can fathom.

Participants: He gives strength to the weary and increases the power of the weak.

Leader: Even youths grow tired and weary, and young men stumble and fall;

Participants: but those who hope in the LORD will renew their strength. They will soar on wings like eagles; they will run and not grow weary, they will walk and not be faint.

For Next Week

Read Mark 15:21–47 in preparation for the next lesson.

Session 7

Jesus Died for Us

(Mark 15:21–47)

Focus

Theme: Punished for My Sin

Law/Gospel Focus

Because of our sin, we deserve God's punishment. Jesus shouldered our punishment and paid our debt by His death on the cross. Jesus restored the broken relationship between people and God to provide us, through faith, eternal life.

Objectives

By the power of the Holy Spirit working through God's Word, we will

1. describe the events just prior to and during Jesus' crucifixion;
2. ponder the magnitude of God's love for us as revealed in the punishment His Son received for our sins;
3. tell others of God's great love for them as revealed in the person and work of Jesus.

Opening Worship

Sing or speak together the following stanzas of "O Dearest Jesus, What Law Have You Broken."

O dearest Jesus, what law have You broken
That such sharp sentence should on You be spoken?
Of what great crime have You to make confession,
What dark transgression?

They crown Your head with thorns, they smite, they scourge You;
With cruel mockings to the cross they urge You;

They give You gall to drink, they still decry You;
They crucify You.

How strange is this great paradox to ponder:
The shepherd dies for sheep who love to wander;
The master pays the debt His servants owe Him,
Who would not know Him.

The sinless Son of God must die in sadness;
The sinful child of man may live in gladness;
We forfeited our lives yet are acquitted;
God is committed!

When, dearest Jesus, at Your throne in heaven
To me the crown of joy at last is given,
Where sweetest hymns Your saints forever raise You,
I too shall praise You!

Introduction

Read Romans 5:6–11. Then complete the following chart.

In the left column, list all of the words that describe people's condition before God because of their sin. Then, in the right column, list the words that indicate the magnitude of God's love for His "enemies."

Words that indicate the condition of people before God because of their sin	Words that indicate the magnitude of God's love for His "enemies"

Now summarize in one or two sentences what God's action on your behalf means to you. Be prepared to share your answer.

In today's lesson, we review that which may be familiar to most of us—the suffering and death of Jesus. We may be inclined to skip this lesson because of its familiarity or because of its brutality. But remember, in this lesson, God reveals to us the depth of His love for us in what has commonly been called "the heart of the Christian faith." So ponder once again the events through which God gives you the forgiveness of sins and eternal life.

Inform

Read Mark 15:21–47 and the following commentary.

About the Text

Death by crucifixion is among the most brutal forms of punishment in human civilization. Even the ancient pagan world regarded execution by a cross with horror. Rulers depended on the threat of crucifixion to maintain public order; people lived in fear and terror of the "stake and crossbar." The Romans used crucifixion as punishment for treason and other heinous crimes. The comedy writer Plautus says, "Go to the cross!" as an expression of utter condemnation.

In the Old Testament, idolaters and blasphemers were stoned to death. They were often then hanged on a tree or a pole as objects of God's wrath and under His curse (Deuteronomy 21:23). When the religious leaders demand crucifixion for Jesus, they not only desire that His death be agonizing but that He bear the full shame of condemnation by God (Galatians 3:13).

"They led Him out to crucify Him" (Mark 15:20). Though exhausted from the trials, interrogations, and scourging, Jesus carries His cross to the city gates. His weariness, however, slows the soldier's progress toward the execution site. A nearby traveler, Simon, is pressed into service. A native of Cyrene, Simon may have been a pilgrim for the Passover feast, in town with his two sons, Alexander and Rufus. (Years later, the family may have shared their remarkable story with believers throughout the Mediterranean world.)

The procession ends at Golgotha. "The Place of the Skull" (v. 22) may refer to the topography (an elevated land mass in the shape of a human skull) or to the routine usage of the site (a place of execution and death). Crucifixion, as with all capital punishment, was done "outside the camp," that is, near but outside the city proper (Leviticus 24:14; Numbers 15:35–38). In this way the wrath of God, as well as the sin of the city/people, was removed (Leviticus 16:27; Hebrews 13:11–14).

Jesus is offered "wine mixed with myrrh" (v. 23), a blend of intoxicants and gum resin to alleviate suffering and extreme pain (see Proverbs 31:6). He refuses, however, to drink anything. Jesus is stripped, fastened to the crossbar, and hoisted up to the top of the wooden scaffold. By custom, the soldiers "inherit" the victim's clothing. For amusement and to pass the time, the soldiers gamble—casting lots has both a sacred and secular context—for the garments, belt, and sandals. (St. John mentions the seamless garment, a valuable "prize"; see 19:23.) In truth, though, they fulfill the words of the Scriptures: "They divide my garments among them and cast lots for my clothing" (Psalm 22:18).

Jesus is crucified around 9 A.M. By Pilate's direct order, the charges are written in three languages and placed conspicuously on the cross: "King of the Jews." (St. John includes the victim's name: "Jesus of Nazareth." The Christian symbol INRI comes from the Latin of the full inscription: *Iesus Nazarenus Rex Iudaeorum,* Jesus of Nazareth, King of the Jews).

The robbers, whose brief dialogue with Jesus is recorded by Luke, were predicted by the prophet Isaiah (53:12). The mocking of the crowds and the religious leaders also fulfills the ancient prophecy (Psalm 22:7–8). While on the cross, Jesus spoke seven times. His first words were not a curse upon His enemies but a prayer for God's forgiveness.

Jesus hangs on the cross for six hours before His death. The sky is dark—a miraculous occurrence—from noon (sixth hour) until 3 P.M. (ninth hour). "The Day of the Lord," a time of judgment, includes supernatural signs in the heavens (Isaiah 13:10; Amos 8:9). Before the first Passover, too, a plague of darkness covered the land as a token of God's wrath upon stubborn Pharaoh and Egypt. The curse of God now, however, falls upon the Son of God, who suffers condemnation on behalf of sinful humanity.

Sometime during the ordeal, Jesus calls out the words of Psalm 22:1 in Aramaic, His native tongue. His prayer reveals the depth of His anguish and experience of isolation—separation from His

Father. "He's calling Elijah" (v. 35) is a mistaken, though plausible, understanding of His cry, especially given the clamor of the crowd—jeers, weeping, wailing, and clashes between the onlookers. Some thought that the prophet Elijah would come to aid the distressed people of God (see Malachi 4:5). The drink offered to Jesus was sour wine, or wine vinegar, a cheap, available intoxicant. Jesus, however, is ready for death.

Jesus "breathed His last" (v. 37). The death is real, not feigned or imagined. The Jerusalem temple had two large veils, one at the entrance to the Holy Place and the other at the entrance to the Holy of Holies (the Most Holy Place). Jesus' death tears the veil at the *inner* sanctuary and thus opens a new and eternal way to the Father (Exodus 26:31–33; Hebrews 9:12).

The earthquake, the splitting of the rocks, the opening of the tombs, and the raising of the saints are part of the supernatural signs at the death of God's Son (Matthew 27:52–53). At this moment, a new community is born. Jesus is the "firstborn" of all who sleep, that is, die, and all who rise to eternal life in His name. All believers, from generations past to the present and beyond, share the hope of a bodily resurrection in Christ.

Mark includes a list of women who followed Jesus from Galilee and who had watched the crucifixion "from a distance" (v. 40). The women were instrumental in providing for the Master and the Twelve during His ministry. They were also faithful disciples.

"As evening approached" (v. 42) refers to the hour before the beginning of the Sabbath. (The new day began at sunset—6:00 P.M.) Joseph of Arimathea is a devout believer in God's promises; he is careful to observe the requirements of Deuteronomy 21:22–23. (The body of a crucified person was not allowed to hang on the cross overnight.) He secures permission to bury Jesus and places the Master in his own new tomb.

Discussing the Text

1. Describe crucifixion; its purpose and horror.

2. What is the significance of the religious leaders' demand for Jesus to be crucified?

3. Why was crucifixion done outside the city?

4. Describe the events during the crucifixion as recorded in Mark's Gospel.

Connect

As you ponder the Lord's suffering and death, consider this Good News: (1)The crucifixion is punishment. God threatens to punish all who disregard His Word, all who violate His will as revealed in the Ten Commandments. And because of His righteousness, God allows no sin to remain unpunished—period. Crucifixion is the cruelest form of punishment. But Jesus willingly accepts the death sentence—even death on a cross! He offers His life as atonement—full reparation—for our offenses.

He pays our debt; He shoulders our punishment. He is our substitute, mediator. In His sacrifice, Jesus restores the broken relationship between humankind and God. His death means reconciliation, peace, and life (Romans 5:11; Colossians 1:22).

(2) Jesus' death was real, marked by brutality and indifference on the part of the soldiers. Too often today, violence seems to have the last word. Moreover, we have become accustomed to, perhaps apathetic toward, the pain and suffering of people in our nation and around the world. God's Law rebukes our selfishness and lack

of concern. Jesus' death, however, demonstrates the extent of His compassion. He is the Good Shepherd, who lays down His life for the flock. "He Himself bore our sins in His body on the tree, so that we might die to sins and live for righteousness" (1 Peter 2:24). The Savior of the world suffers for the world, so that in Him we might escape the pain and suffering of eternal death. Of course, everyone still dies. But through Christ, God gives us the assurance of His presence at all stages of life, even when we stand at death's portal. We are fully forgiven and blessed forever.

1. Describe the significance of Jesus' crucifixion for you.

2. Although you will still physically die, what comfort does Jesus' death and resurrection give to you?

3. Which events of the Passion account are most meaningful to you? Why?

Vision

To Do This Week

Family Connection

1. Reread Mark's account of the crucifixion during family devotion time. Then read the crucifixion account from Matthew, Luke, and John. List the events on a sheet of paper.

2. Have each member of the family share what Jesus' crucifixion means to her or him.

3. Ask, "What should occur if someone does something wrong?"

Most members of the family will agree that people should be punished if they do something wrong. Then remind family members that they deserved punishment because of their sins. God, in His love for each of us, had His only Son punished for our sin. We receive that which Jesus deserved because He lived a perfect life—eternal life.

4. Draw pictures depicting the events leading up to and including the crucifixion.

Personal Reflection

1. Meditate on the events surrounding the crucifixion of Jesus. Consider the brutality of crucifixion; brutality that you deserved because of your sin. Praise God for sending His only Son to take the punishment you deserved.

2. Pray that God would provide you opportunities this week to tell a friend or loved one about the magnitude of His love revealed in the person and work of Jesus.

3. Review the words of "O Dearest Jesus, What Law Have You Broken" during your personal devotion time.

Closing Worship

Once again, speak or sing the stanzas of "O Dearest Jesus, What Law Have You Broken," found in the Opening Worship activity.

For Next Week

Read Mark 16:1–8 in preparation for the next lesson.

Session 8

Jesus Rises from the Dead

(Mark 16:1–8 and parallels)

Focus

Theme: Dependent Upon

Law/Gospel Focus

Death is the tragic consequence of sin. Jesus confronted death in order to redeem (purchase back) His people from death. By the power of the almighty God, Jesus overcomes death to assure us of His forgiveness and eternal life. We confess by the power of the Holy Spirit that we are completely dependent upon Jesus for our salvation.

Objectives

By the power of the Holy Spirit working through God's Word, we will
1. trace the events of Jesus' resurrection as recorded in the Gospel accounts;
2. compare and contrast the different Gospel accounts of Jesus' resurrection;
3. share what Jesus' resurrection means for me.

Opening Worship

Read the collect for the resurrection of our Lord.

Almighty God the Father, through Your only-begotten Son Jesus Christ You have overcome death and opened the gate of everlasting life to us. Grant that we, who celebrate with joy the day of our Lord's resurrection, may be raised from the death of sin by Your life-giving Spirit; through Jesus Christ, our Lord, who lives and reigns with You and the Holy Spirit, one God, now and forever. Amen.

Introduction

"I am dependent upon ..."

1. Complete this sentence starter with as many endings as you can think of that relate to your life.

2. What occurs when something you depend upon proves to be less than reliable?

In today's lesson, we apply to our lives that which is completely reliable and on which we can always depend—that because Jesus lives, we too will live.

Inform

Read Mark 16:1–8 and the following commentary.

About the Text

"The third day He rose again from the dead." In the Apostles' Creed the church confesses the greatest miracle of all time. The collective witness of the Gospels, as well as the other writings of the New Testament, is "The Lord is risen!" Christian faith is rooted in, and utterly dependent upon, the resurrection of Jesus for the life and salvation of the world.

The story of the resurrection cannot, of course, be separated from the death and burial of Jesus. The crucifixion takes place on Friday; Jesus dies around 3:00 P.M. Joseph of Arimathea, a devout member of the Sanhedrin (the ruling council), requests permission from Pilate to take and bury the body. As a "prominent member" of the council (Mark 15:43), Joseph has access to Pilate.

Pilate is surprised that Jesus has died so quickly. Many victims lingered for days, requiring the constant presence of a military guard. Joseph's request is urgent; he wishes to provide a prompt, but proper, burial for Jesus before the beginning of the Sabbath. (The Jewish "day" began at sunset; the Sabbath observance lasted therefore from Friday evening to Saturday evening.)

Pilate's consent allows Joseph to remove Jesus' body from the cross, make the necessary arrangements, and place the Lord in the tomb. "A stone against the entrance" (Mark 15:46) lends dignity to the hasty arrangements. It also served as a "guard" against unauthorized entry into the tomb (see Matthew 27:62–66). Some of the women who followed Jesus note the exact place "where He was laid" (Mark 15:47) and return home to prepare spices for the full burial after the Sabbath.

The women (and disciples) rest on Saturday, according to the command of God. Early Sunday morning, Mary Magdalene, Mary the mother of James, Salome, and Joanna (Luke 24:10) start out toward the tomb to anoint Jesus' body with the mixture of spices and fragrant oils. Like the disciples, the women have not understood God's plan to raise the Messiah to life on the third day. They focus on the work at hand and wonder how they will be able to enter the tomb.

Sometime before the women reach the site, however, the extraordinary sequence of events begins.

1. Jesus rises from the dead. His body, once truly dead, is "made alive" and renewed to new, eternal life. He destroys the power of Satan, sin, and death.

2. The angel of the Lord descends from heaven. He rolls back the stone and opens the entrance to the tomb (Matthew 28:2).

3. A "violent earthquake" occurs in the graveyard and throughout Jerusalem (Matthew 28:2). Many saints—God's people—are raised from death to life to testify to the resurrection (Matthew 27:53).

4. The guards at the tomb see the angel(s), whose appearance is like lightning. They fall down in terror and remain motionless—most likely in a state of shock. Later, the soldiers recover and return to Jerusalem to make their report to the chief priests and council. (See Matthew 28:11–15.)

5. The women reach the tomb; they enter but do not see Jesus.

6. The angels appear and announce the resurrection of Jesus to the women. (Luke reports two angels in the tomb; Mark and Matthew mention only the spokesman, perhaps the "archangel.")

7. The angels instruct the women to tell the disciples that Jesus is risen.

Each Gospel account presents an important piece of the whole Easter story, with distinctive truths about Jesus' appearances to His disciples.

Mark emphasizes the women's sheer surprise at the Lord's resurrection. The angel's announcement provokes at first only fear and bewilderment. The women flee from the heavenly messenger and from the tomb site. On the road home—that is, toward the place where the disciples are gathered—they say "nothing to anyone" (Mark 16:8). Perhaps they stopped to discuss with one another the Lord's teaching about His crucifixion and His promise to rise from the dead. Mark, however, concludes the resurrection account with the women's deep consternation at their unexpected discovery. In this way, Mark draws attention to the proclamation of the Word—the teaching and preaching about the Lord's death and resurrection. The church of Mark's day and today hears and believes the Gospel not on the basis of regular appearances of the risen Lord, but on the basis of His promises. Preachers and teachers carry on the Savior's commission to share the Good News (see Mark 1:14–15).

Matthew furnishes vital information on the circumstances of the Lord's resurrection, but in particular describes the Lord's first appearance to the women. As in Mark, the women flee from the tomb "afraid yet filled with joy" (Matthew 28:8). But Matthew immediately reports that Jesus meets the women on their way to tell the disciples (just as the angel commanded; see Matthew 28:7).

The risen Lord bestows His greeting and comfort. He reiterates the instruction to the disciples, "Go to Galilee." Sometime before His ascension, Jesus meets the disciples on a Galilean mountain. There He teaches and gives the great commission (Matthew 28:16–20).

Luke provides further detail on the appearances to the women and the later appearances to the other disciples. Luke specifically states that after the angel's announcement, the women "remembered His words" (24:8). Though overwhelmed with emotion, they nevertheless believe the Good News. Luke does not report the Lord's appearance to the women on the road; the event is perhaps implied in their faith. Instead, Luke focuses upon the apostles' reaction to their report: the apostles "did not believe the women, because their words seemed to them like nonsense" (Luke 24:11). Luke briefly narrates Peter's swift trip to the tomb and his uncertainty over the events of the day. Luke also presents the story of the Emmaus disciples (24:13–35) and the appearances to the disciples (24:36–49).

John focuses upon Mary Magdalene as representative of the women who journeyed to the tomb and later met the risen Lord. The reason, perhaps, is Mary's humble beginning in the community and her utter devotion to Jesus. (Luke 8:2 reports that Mary had seven demons cast out from within her; she was eternally grateful to her Lord and Savior.) With the other women, Mary reports the Lord's resurrection to Peter and the "beloved disciple" (traditionally, John). The two apostles run to the tomb, but do not find Jesus. Mary, too, returns to the tomb. She is weeping as she peers into the grave site, where two angels sit. Her response to the angels' question is evidence of her love and reverence for the Master. She does not, however, recognize Jesus. When the Lord speaks her name, His identity is sure. He is her dear teacher, Messiah, and Savior. Jesus tells Mary to report His resurrection appearance to the apostles, and she quickly returns to share the Good News.

(For the story of the apostles and Thomas, see Lesson 9.)

Discussing the Text

1. Why is the resurrection of Jesus considered the greatest miracle of all time? What does the miracle of the resurrection mean for you?

2. List the extraordinary sequence of events.

3. Each of the Gospel accounts presents an important piece of the Easter story. Summarize the emphases of each of the Gospel accounts.
- Mark

- Matthew

- Luke

- John

Connect

In considering the Good News of the Lord's resurrection, focus upon these applications for your life. (1) Death is the consequence of sin (Genesis 2:17; Romans 5:12; 1 Corinthians 15:21–22). This axiom *is* true: "In a perfect world, no one dies." The thought offers little comfort, though, because all people are born sinful and sin daily throughout their lives. Sin is the stark reality, and sin always pays a dreadful wage: death (Romans 6:23)! The Good News of Jesus' resurrection revolves around the victory over sin, death, and Satan, as well as the power for new life. The crucified Messiah is now the risen Lord.

By the grace of God, Jesus confronts death—He did "taste death" (Hebrews 2:9)—in order to redeem His people from their slavery. By the almighty power of God, He then overcomes death to assure His people of forgiveness and eternal life in His name.

(2) The resurrection also reveals Jesus as the compassionate Lord, who transforms fear and unbelief into confidence in His Word. Throughout the Old Testament, God's prophets called the people to repentance and faith. But the people often ignored the Lord's Word, despite His miraculous signs: "they did not believe in God or trust in His deliverance" (Psalm 78:22). The message of the angels and the inescapable truth of His appearances is that "He has risen, just as He said" (Matthew 28:6). As He comes to His disciples on Easter day and in the weeks after His resurrection, Jesus shares His word of comfort and hope. He is Savior and Lord.

1. Summarize what the good news of Jesus' resurrection means for you and your life.

2. How does the resurrection reveal Jesus as the compassionate Lord? What does this compassion mean for you in your life? In your death?

Vision

To Do This Week

Family Connection

1. Review each of the resurrection accounts. List the significant events from each.

2. Discuss what the resurrection of Jesus means for you. Let each family member share what the resurrection means for her or him.

3. Send Easter cards to friends and family members. Consider creating a family Easter card that emphasizes what the good news of the resurrection means to your family.

4. Consider having a family Easter celebration. Invite friends and loved ones to celebrate with you.

Personal Reflection

1. During your personal devotion time, read the resurrection account from each of the Gospels.

2. Offer prayers of thanksgiving and praise for the victory Jesus proclaimed in His resurrection for you over sin, death, and the power of the devil.

3. Share with a friend what the resurrection means to you.

Closing Worship

Close with the alternate collect for the Resurrection of our Lord.

O God, for our redemption You have given Your only-begotten Son to the death of the cross, and by His glorious resurrection You have delivered us from the power of our enemy. Therefore grant that all our sin may be drowned through daily repentance and that day by day a new man may arise to live before You in righteousness and purity forever; through Jesus Christ, Your Son, our Lord, who lives and reigns with You and the Holy Spirit, one God, now and forever. Amen.

For Next Week

Read John 20:19–31 and 1 John 5:1–6 in preparation for the next lesson.

Session 9

Jesus Made Us His Children: Jesus Appears to Thomas

(John 20:19–31; 1 John 5:1–6)

Focus

Theme: Seeing Is Believing

Law/Gospel Focus

Because of sin, we desire to live "by sight"; that is, we rely upon our senses, our talents, and our resources to succeed. We count on our strengths or intellect to solve problems that occur at home and at work. Yet Jesus' presence creates faith. His Word calls forth and strengthens faith. Since He is alive, risen from the dead, He becomes the focus of our life and gives us strength to live by faith enabling us to call upon Him at all times, "My Lord and my God!"

Objectives

By the power of the Holy Spirit working through God's Word, we will
1. summarize the resurrection events;
2. confess that we, like Thomas, rely on our sight rather than faith;
3. praise God that through His Word He strengthens faith in the crucified and risen Jesus, thus empowering us to live by faith.

Opening Worship

Speak together the following stanzas of "O Sons and Daughters of the King."

O sons and daughters of the King,
Whom heav'nly hosts in glory sing,
Today the grave has lost its sting! Alleluia!

That Easter morn, at break of day,
The faithful women went their way
To seek the tomb where Jesus lay. Alleluia!

An angel clad in white they see,
Who sits and speaks unto the three,
"Your Lord will go to Galilee." Alleluia!

That night the apostles met in fear;
Among them came their master dear
And said, "My peace be with you here." Alleluia!

When Thomas first the tidings heard
That they had seen the risen Lord,
He doubted the disciples' word. Alleluia!

"My pierced side, O Thomas, see,
And look upon My hands, My feet;
Not faithless but believing be." Alleluia!

No longer Thomas then denied;
He saw the feet, the hands, the side;
"You are my Lord and God!" he cried. Alleluia!

Introduction

"Seeing is believing."

1. Describe a situation that caused you or someone you know to speak these words.

2. What human characteristic does this phrase illustrate?

This familiar saying summarizes a basic human instinct: to depend upon ourselves—our talents, treasures, skills, and abilities. In this lesson, you may at first be inclined to judge Thomas harshly for his doubt and questioning. But if we are honest, we must admit that at times we all live by a "seeing is believing" attitude. We forget that our lives belong to the one who created us and recreated us through Holy Baptism.

Inform

Read John 20:19–31; 1 John 5:1–6; and the commentary that follows.

About the Text

Late in the evening on the day of Jesus' resurrection, the disciples gather together at a private home in Jerusalem. They meet quietly, secretly, because to all appearances their hopes are gone. The Master is still dead, they believe. The Roman governor Pontius Pilate, at the instigation of the religious leaders and the crowd, signed the execution order. In a matter of hours, Jesus was taken away and crucified. The disciples know that they, too, are now vulnerable. They can be excluded from the synagogue for confessing the Lord's name (John 9:22). Or they can be arrested, charged, and punished.

Jesus comes in the midst of their fears. The doors are locked, but Jesus appears in their presence. He is risen, victorious, glorified. The Savior of the world, once slain, is alive and draws near to His disciples in the flesh. He lives and rules as the Lord of life.

"Peace be with you" (v. 19). From Jesus, the words are not simply a traditional greeting among friends, but a declaration of wholeness, well-being, and completeness. He shares His peace (John 16:33). He calls forth faith. He gives His forgiveness and salvation.

Jesus shows His "hands and side" (v. 20). It is the same body, the same flesh and blood raised from death to life. The disciples see that Jesus is not present in some "mystical" or "spiritual" sense, but in person. The wounds inflicted by the Roman soldiers, wounds caused by nails and spears, are evident, but no longer mortal. Jesus is with His followers and friends. Nothing else could bring more joy.

After a second blessing of "Peace be with you," the Lord confers His mission upon the disciples. In His priestly prayer before His death, Jesus addressed the heavenly Father, "As You have sent Me into the world, I have sent them into the world" (John 17:18). With the work of salvation finished, the Good News must be announced. Jesus breathes upon the apostles to bestow the Holy Spirit. (The language is reminiscent of God's creative breath at the first creation; see Genesis 2:7.) The Spirit is at work to re-create God's people for ministry.

"Receive the Holy Spirit" (v. 22). The gift of the Spirit awaited Jesus' glorification and His return to the Father (John 7:39; 15:26; 16:7). There is, then, an intimate connection between the resurrection and the Spirit's descent upon the disciples. (The Book of Acts relates the story of the first Pentecost). Because Jesus is risen from the dead and holds the "keys" of forgiveness and life, He sends the Spirit to empower His church—through the chosen apostles—to continue the mission. It is, of course, His authority and strength behind the call to forgive repentant sinners and to withhold forgiveness from unrepentant sinners.

The apostles, as representatives of Christ, carry out their charge only by His grace; they, too, are simply forgiven sinners. Yet they serve God's people by divine commission and power. On the Last Day, God will confirm what the Church proclaims: that all who come to Jesus in repentance and trust receive full, free forgiveness and eternal life.

Thomas is a bold, inquisitive follower. He illustrates the struggle of faith in a world dominated by sight and sound and touch. For some reason, he is not present with the Twelve on Easter Sunday. (The designation "the Twelve" was traditional; Judas's death reduced the number to 11.) The apostles' claim, "We have seen the Lord!" is, therefore, not persuasive. Thomas needs to see and hear the Lord *in person*. He will be convinced only when he grasps the hands punctured by nails and feels the flesh pierced by the Roman spear. In many respects, Thomas speaks for all disciples, including the apostles, who hours before had doubted the testimony of the women (Luke 24:11).

On the next Sunday, the disciples again meet together in seclusion. As before, Jesus suddenly appears and shares His word of blessing. His focus now, however, is Thomas; His words converge directly upon the apostle's doubts and fears. The evidence is clear. The nail marks and wounds are convincing. Thomas responds as the Spirit moves him: "My Lord and My God!" (v. 28). His confession of faith leaves no doubt. Jesus is alive; He is the risen Lord and eternal God.

Thomas ascribes to Jesus all the attributes of God the Father. The perfect bond between Father and Son is complete: "that all may honor the Son just as they honor the Father" (John 5:23). The sacrifice of the Son of God on the cross has, in the Father's eyes, redeemed the world once for all. The triumph of the Son of God in the resurrection has also, by the Father's will and plan, brought full salvation and life to all who believe.

Jesus addresses Thomas, but His words apply to all disciples: "Blessed are those who have not seen and yet have believed" (20:29). The appearances of the risen Lord are important—especially for the apostles at the beginning of their mission. Yet ultimately it is the Gospel preached and taught to generation after generation that creates and nurtures saving faith. The Gospel is power (Romans 1:16). Christ is truly present in His Word and in His "visible Word," Baptism and the Lord's Supper.

St. John provides a fitting close to the resurrection accounts. Like the other miraculous signs in the Gospel, the story of Jesus' dying and rising to life aims simply to proclaim Christ, the Son of God. The whole document, written in faith, is designed to call forth and strengthen faith. Believing in Jesus results in life in His name. It is pure Gospel—"in a nutshell" (see also John 3:16).

Discussing the Text

1. What caused the disciples to gather together in fear?

2. What is the significance of Jesus' words "Peace be with you"?

3. How does Thomas demonstrate the struggle of faith in a world dominated by sight, sound, and touch?

4. What is the significance of Thomas' confession of faith, "My Lord and my God!"?

5. Why is St. John's close to the resurrection accounts fitting?

Connect

The lesson revolves around two themes with strong application for your life. (1) St. Paul notes, "We live by faith, not by sight" (2 Corinthians 5:7). For the most part, though, we desire to live "by sight." We rely upon our senses, our talents, and our resources to succeed in the world. We count on our strength or intellect to make our way through problems and challenges at work and home. God's word of judgment is clear: "Cursed is the one who trusts in man, who depends on flesh for his strength" (Jeremiah 17:5). Lack of faith in God's promise and power but, above all, rejection of God's promise and power, is sin. Yet Jesus' presence creates faith. His Word calls forth and strengthens faith. Because He is alive, risen from the dead, He is the one focus of our faith and worship. His mighty power, seen today in His Word and sacraments, gives us strength.

(2) The resurrection provides the power for the Lord's apostles to continue His ministry. They are given the same commission as their Master: to call all people to repentance and faith in God's Messiah, the Savior of the world. First, they proclaim the Law—God's righteousness, human sinfulness, and the prospect of punishment and death. Then they proclaim the Gospel—Jesus died for our sins and was raised to life for our justification (Romans 4:25). His death

and resurrection, then, are the focal points of all Christian preaching and teaching. But strength for the task comes from Christ alone; by His Word and authority, the apostles proclaim forgiveness and *forgive* the sins of repentant believers.

We hear God's absolution in Word and Sacrament.

1. What is the significance of St. Paul's statement "We live by faith, not by sight"?

2. Give specific examples of times when you have lived by sight, not by faith.

3. Thanks be to God! Jesus' death on the cross paid the price for all of your sins, including your sinful doubts. What does the forgiveness won by Jesus on the cross mean for you as you struggle to "live by faith, not by sight"?

4. How do we continue to live out Jesus' commission today?

Vision

To Do This Week

Family Connection

1. Review the resurrection accounts from John's Gospel. Ask, "What is unique about these accounts?"

2. Confess to each other the tendency for all people to live by sight, not by faith. Assure one another of the forgiveness Jesus

merited for you on the cross. Pray that the Holy Spirit working through God's Word would enable you to live by faith, not by sight.

3. Have each member of the family think of one of the resurrection accounts, possibly her or his favorite. Then play 20 questions to see if the other family members can guess the account.

Personal Reflection

1. Confess your sinful impulse to live by sight and not by faith. For this and all other sins, Jesus went to the cross.

2. Meditate on the meaning of the resurrection for you and your life—here on earth and into eternity.

3. Share with a friend the confession "My Lord and my God!" as you tell about God's love for you in Christ Jesus.

Closing Worship

Speak together the last two stanzas of "O Sons and Daughters of the King."

> How blest are they who have not seen
> And yet whose faith has constant been,
> For they eternal life shall win. Alleluia!
>
> On this most holy day of days
> Be laud and jubilee and praise:
> To God your hearts and voices raise. Alleluia!

For Next Week

Read Luke 24:36–49 in preparation for the next lesson.

Session 10

Jesus Gives Us Peace: Jesus Appears to His Disciples

(Luke 24:36–49)

Focus

Theme: Peace Be with You!

Law/Gospel Focus

Recognizing our sin, we stand before God in terror. But Jesus, in His love for us, comes to us in our fear and speaks words of comfort, "Peace be with you!" For Jesus stood before God in our place and received the punishment we deserved because of our sin as He suffered and died on the cross. The victory He proclaimed at His resurrection is our victory. He replaces our fear of death with peace as we look forward to eternal life.

Objectives

By the power of the Holy Spirit working through God's Word, we will

1. describe the reason for the fear the disciples had when they saw Jesus;
2. explain how Jesus shares with us the peace He shared with His disciples;
3. share the peace that Jesus gives to us with others.

Opening Worship

Pray together the collect for Easter evening:

Almighty God the Father, through Your only-begotten Son Jesus Christ You have overcome death and opened the gate of everlasting life to us. Grant that we, who celebrate with joy the day of our Lord's resurrection, may be raised

> from the death of sin by Your life-giving Spirit; through Jesus Christ, our Lord, who lives and reigns with You and the Holy Spirit, one God, now and forever. Amen.

Introduction

"I just want a little *peace* and quiet."
"May he rest in *peace.*"
"We should live in *peace.*"

We often use the word *peace* to describe the way in which we desire to live.

1. Describe the *peace* in which people desire to live.

2. In what do people often seek *peace*?

3. Why is *peace* so often fleeting?

In today's lesson, Jesus offers His disciples peace. The peace that Jesus gives is a peace that "transcends all understanding" (Philippians 4:7). It is peace with God, peace in the knowledge that sins are forgiven, peace in knowing that we will live forever with God, peace in the fact that "[nothing] will be able to separate us from the love of God that is in Christ Jesus our Lord" (Romans 8:39).

Inform

Read Luke 24:36–49 and the following commentary.

About the Text

As evening came that first Easter Sunday, the eleven apostles and the other followers of Jesus, men and women, were more and more convinced that the grave was empty because Jesus had risen. But they had little understanding as to just what that meant. People in those days generally believed that the souls of the dead were able to roam the earth. There was a great fear of ghosts. However, it was unthinkable that a dead person could make bodily appearances.

Yet that is exactly what Jesus did: with his glorified body he appears to Mary Magdalene, to Peter, to the Emmaus disciples, and here to the group which has assembled. His greeting is the familiar: "Peace be with you." It is a word they all need to hear, for they are understandably filled with fear.

Jesus first wants to convince his disciples they are not seeing a ghost but a real, live person. He shows them his hands and feet still marked with the wounds he suffered. He invites them to touch him to demonstrate that he has flesh and blood and is no ghost. Finally he eats a piece of broiled fish before their doubting eyes. There is a great struggle going on in their hearts between the joy of believing and the dread of being deceived. So faith wrestles with doubt in the Christian's heart.

Not only is this the same person who ate and drank with his disciples during his earthly ministry, his message is the same. Jesus reminds them of how his entire ministry is a fulfillment of the Old Testament Scriptures. The first public sermon preached by Jesus as recorded by Luke began with this thematic statement: "Today this Scripture is fulfilled in your hearing" (4:21). Jesus moves through the various books of the Old Testament opening the minds of his disciples to show how all has been fulfilled in himself. The Old Testament is promise; the New Testament is fulfillment. The message is the same: repentance and the forgiveness of sins. ...

Jesus concludes by giving to his followers a command and a promise. Their task will be to preach to all nations, witnessing to all they had seen and heard. It is an awesome assignment which

Jesus gives; but along with it comes the promise that the disciples will be "clothed with power from on high." The book of the Acts of the Apostles (also written by Luke) tells the story of how the Holy Spirit empowered the disciples to go with the gospel. The journey of Jesus ended in Jerusalem; the mission of the church will begin in that same city and finally reach to the ends of the earth.

From Victor H. Prange, *The People's Bible: Luke.* © 1988 Northwestern Publishing House. Used by permission. (Reprinted by CPH as *The People's Bible Commentary: Luke*, 1992, pp. 263–64.)

Discussing the Text

1. Although the 11 apostles and other followers of Jesus were convinced that Jesus had risen from the dead, what caused them to misunderstand the meaning of this event?

2. Why was Jesus' greeting, "Peace be with you," particularly appropriate for the disciples to hear?

3. Describe the events involved in Jesus' appearance to His disciples. Why were these events significant? What did they teach the disciples?

4. What command and promise did Jesus give to His disciples?

Connect

As you reflect upon the resurrection appearance, remember our human need and God's rich provision in Christ. (1) The kingdom of God does not come about by human aspirations or efforts. We often impose our selfish expectations and demands upon God's purpose. We concentrate on the minor issues; God focuses upon the major problem: "your iniquities have separated you from your God" (Isaiah 59:2). God's kingdom, then, centers in grace. " 'Not by might nor by power, but by My Spirit,' says the LORD Almighty" (Zechariah 4:6). God's purpose is now accomplished in Christ. The Lord Almighty has acted decisively to save sinful humanity from sin and death. Jesus dies; He rises to life. The cross and resurrection fulfill God's plan and usher in His kingdom of mercy and forgiveness.

(2) At times, even believers are "foolish" and "slow of heart" (Luke 24:25). We lack understanding; we lack the strength and resolve to hear the Word regularly. Our sinful nature resists the gracious call of God's Spirit to grow in faith and knowledge of the Savior. Yet Jesus opens our eyes to see the one hope of salvation. Jesus brings truth because He is the truth. He reveals the Father's plan in His life, death, and resurrection. All Scripture conveys and communicates God's saving work in Christ.

1. How is Jesus' command and promise to the disciples still important for us today?

2. How does that which Jesus accomplished through His death on the cross and proclaimed through His resurrection give you peace?

3. How are we at times "foolish" and "slow of heart"? How does Jesus respond to our foolishness?

Vision

To Do This Week

Family Connection

1. Reread the events of Jesus' appearing to the disciples. Ask, "How might you respond if Jesus appeared today to you?" Let family members share. Then say, "Jesus continues to appear to us through God's Word. Why is this important?"

2. Send Easter greetings in the form of letters or cards to friends and loved ones. Put this message in each of the greetings: "Peace be with you." Then illustrate the words. Let each member of the family write a short paragraph to include in the greeting that describes the peace that Jesus gives them.

3. Review Jesus' command and promise. Consider how you as a family might follow Jesus' command. Then discuss how Jesus' promise empowers you to do as He commands.

Personal Reflection

1. Reread the Easter account. Meditate on the meaning it has for you.

2. Pray that the Holy Spirit would empower and equip you to follow Jesus' command. Give thanks to God for the promise Jesus gives to be with you always.

3. Share the words "Peace be with you" or simply "Peace" as your greeting this week. Consider how you will respond when people ask you the meaning of the greeting. This may provide a tremendous opportunity for you to share the peace you have because of what God has accomplished for you through Christ.

Closing Worship

Speak together the words of Psalm 100.

> Shout for joy to the LORD, all the earth.
>> Worship the LORD with gladness;
>> come before Him with joyful songs.
> Know that the LORD is God.
>> It is He who made us, and we are His;
>> we are His people, the sheep of His pasture.
> Enter His gates with thanksgiving
>> and His courts with praise;
>> give thanks to Him and praise His name.
> For the LORD is good and His love endures forever;
>> His faithfulness continues through all generations.

For Next Week

Read John 10:1–18 in preparation for next week's study.

Session 11

Our Good Shepherd Cares for Us

(John 10:1–18)

Focus

Theme: Me, a Sheep?

Law/Gospel Focus

All people are by nature lost sheep. We choose our own paths that lead to separation and ultimately destruction. We stray from the flock, wandering aimlessly amid the ravages of life, even though we have known our Shepherd's care and goodness. Jesus reminds us that as the Good Shepherd, He is also the Gentle Savior who came to earth to rescue His people by laying down His life so that we, His sheep, may live assured of His eternal safety.

Objectives

By the power of the Holy Spirit working through God's Word, we will

1. describe how we are lost sheep;
2. explain how Jesus is our Good Shepherd who rescued us from the clutches of evil so that we might live in His eternal safety;
3. share Jesus' love with other sheep who have strayed.

Opening Worship

Pray together the collect for the Fourth Sunday of Easter:

Almighty God, merciful Father, since You have wakened from death the Shepherd of Your sheep, grant us Your Holy Spirit that we may know the voice of our Shepherd and follow Him that sin and death may never pluck us out of Your hand; through Jesus Christ, our Lord, who lives and reigns with You and the Holy Spirit, one God, now and forever. Amen.

Introduction

"You are a sheep!" Although we have rarely, if ever, heard these words spoken to us or used these words ourselves, calling someone a sheep is a very derogatory remark. Consider the facts: sheep are not bright; they wander off unknowingly into danger; they are helpless when they encounter a problem; they are easily led away from the flock.

1. How are you like a sheep, particularly as you consider your relationship with God?

2. What danger do you and all people face because of "sheep-like" characteristics?

In today's lesson, Jesus, the Good Shepherd, speaks to us words of comfort and encouragement. For the Good Shepherd not only offers us abundant life here on earth but also the promise of eternal life with Him.

Inform

Read John 10:1–18 and the commentary that follows.

About the Text

Shepherds were an integral part of ancient society and daily life. Because sheep were among the most common—and important—domestic animals in many parts of the Middle East, every family and settlement needed reliable shepherds. The work was difficult, at times dangerous, but crucial for the survival of the community. Good shepherds were faithful, brave, and diligent in protecting and caring for their flocks.

The image of the shepherd provides a natural analogy for describing the love, compassion, and care of God toward His chosen people. Throughout the Bible, God is portrayed as a gentle Shepherd who directs, strengthens, comforts, and rescues His flock. The Lord God is the Shepherd of Israel, the nation He has chosen from all peoples of the earth. Though Israel strays like helpless sheep, God redeems and restores the wandering flock. He promises to be present, to tend and lead His people amid the hazards of their journey through life.

The picture of God as Shepherd finds fulfillment in Jesus, the Good Shepherd and Savior of the world. Early Christians proclaimed the Good News that the heavenly Father sent His only Son into the world to gather together the lost children of God. Jesus is the Messiah, through whom the gracious rule of God is revealed in humble glory—suffering, sacrifice, and death.

In His resurrection, Jesus is exalted as Shepherd King, who governs and guides His Church in love and almighty power. The "old era" of law, sin, and death comes to an end in Christ, for He calls forth His disciples—His flock—to life eternal in His name.

In John 10, Jesus speaks to the disciples and Jews who had witnessed the healing of the blind man. Some Pharisees are also present, whom Jesus rebukes as unbelievers. Because the religious leaders refuse to acknowledge God's Son in human flesh, the Lord teaches in parables. Only the "eyes of faith" see His meaning and purpose.

The "figure of speech" (v. 6) contains six central features: (1) the thief/robber; (2) the shepherd; (3) the watchman; (4) the gate; (5) the sheep; and (6) the stranger.

In ancient times, a flock of sheep was usually herded into a sheep pen for the night. Many pens were permanent enclosures surrounded by stone walls, with a single gate or door as entranceway. Several different flocks might spend the night in one enclosure, under the supervision of the watchman posted near the entrance. The shepherds came in the morning and were admitted by the watchman. Each shepherd knew his sheep and was in turn known to the sheep.

A thief or robber might attempt to "call" to the sheep from outside the pen, or possibly to climb the wall to steal part of the flock. But the sheep are not deceived by the intruder's voice. Nor can the sheep be taken from under the careful eye of the watchman. The sheep know their master and will not follow a stranger.

The shepherd has free and complete access to the flock. "He calls His own sheep by name" (v. 3) refers to the practice of giving pet names to individual animals (e.g., Long Ears, White Nose, and the like). At grazing time, the shepherd walks in front of the flock, calling, beckoning, and leading the sheep to safe pastures. Though someone else calls, the sheep still follow their master, for they recognize only the voice of the true shepherd.

Because the crowd does not understand, Jesus applies the parable directly to His life and mission. He is "the gate for the sheep," (v. 7), the one door to eternal salvation (see John 14:6). The "thieves and robbers" (v. 8) are the false messiahs and prophets of the past and the present, who "steal and kill and destroy" (v. 10) the people of God. Jesus is the "good shepherd" (v. 11), who comes in the name of the Father to give life "to the full" (v. 10) to all believers. His role is servant, sentinel, above all, Savior. His appointment with the cross is all part of a good shepherd's care: to lay down his life for the sheep. A "hired hand" (v. 12) does not protect and save the sheep. When danger threatens, he leaves the flock defenseless and at extreme risk. The hired hand works simply for the wages of the day and his own interests. The true shepherd invests his life in the safety and contentment of each individual sheep.

Jesus shares this sacrificial love with His people. His purpose, forged in the heart of the Father, is to redeem His lost sheep throughout the world, Jews and Gentiles alike. He knows, He saves, He calls each one by name. Though scattered to many different places, the sheep are gathered together—one flock under one Shepherd.

Discussing the Text

1. Describe the importance of the vocation of shepherd in ancient society.

2. Why is the image of a shepherd an appropriate analogy to describe God?

3. The figure of speech described by Jesus has six central figures. What are these central figures? How is each important in understanding the theological significance of Jesus' parable?

4. How does Jesus directly apply the parable to His life and mission? Why does Jesus do this?

Connect

As you reflect upon the blessings of our Good Shepherd, consider these truths. (1) All people, by nature, are lost sheep (Isaiah 53:6; Jeremiah 50:6). We choose our own paths—paths that lead to separation and destruction. We stray from the flock, wandering aimlessly amid the ravages of life, even though we have known our Maker's care and goodness. Sometimes we even get lost in the fray, pushed out and around by "care less" people. We feel utterly alone—abandoned and without protection. Jesus reminds us that the Good Shepherd is also the Gentle Savior. He comes to rescue His people. He gives His life as the sacrifice for their eternal safety and contentment.

(2) God's people face danger on many different fronts. Most visible, however, are the "thieves and robbers," who come simply to "steal and kill and destroy." Believers individually and the church

collectively will always be assaulted by false prophets and teachers; we hear others calling us to leave the Shepherd. In sharp contrast, Jesus brings full life. By faith we are connected to His truth, His power. Because He has given His own life for us, He will lead us through many temptations and struggles to our heavenly home.

(3) Our world is fractured into hundreds of pieces: nations, states, cities, towns, races, ethnic groups, tribes, political parties, and so on. Only Jesus brings this diversity into unity. Though scattered, His church is "one flock," gathered under "one shepherd." At the end of time, He will bring all His people together: "one Lord, one faith, one baptism; one God and Father of all" (Ephesians 4:5–6).

1. Which of the three truths described above do you think is most significant? Why?

2. In your own words, use the sheep and shepherd analogy to describe you and your life of faith.

3. Describe some analogies from today's society that would convey the message described in the sheep/shepherd analogy.

4. What comfort does the Good Shepherd provide to you?

5. Why is the one flock concept so important for us to affirm in such a diverse society?

Vision

To Do This Week

Family Connection

1. Draw a family picture showing the important facts told by Jesus in the parable of the shepherd. Or draw a picture of the Good Shepherd that shows what Jesus did and is doing for His sheep today.

2. Create a sheep collage using cotton balls, glue, and markers and/or colored pencils. Write the name of each family member under each of the sheep. Then label the poster "We are sheep under the care of the Good Shepherd."

3. Read Psalm 23. Discuss the blessings the Good Shepherd provides for His sheep.

Personal Reflection

1. Review the parable of the shepherd. Then read Psalm 23. What connections can you make between that which Jesus teaches and that which David describes in the psalm?

2. Confess your sinful sheeplike characteristics. Praise God for the forgiveness obtained for you by the Good Shepherd, who laid down His life for you.

3. Share the story of the Good Shepherd with a friend or loved one. Consider creating a modern analogy that describes the truth revealed in John 10.

Closing Worship

Read Psalm 23.

> The LORD is my shepherd, I shall not be in want.
>> He makes me lie down in green pastures,
> He leads me beside quiet waters,
>> He restores my soul.

He guides me in paths of righteousness
>> for His name's sake.
Even though I walk
>> through the valley of the shadow of death,
I will fear no evil,
>> for You are with me;
Your rod and Your staff,
>> they comfort me.

You prepare a table before me
>> in the presence of my enemies.
You anoint my head with oil;
>> my cup overflows.
Surely goodness and love will follow me
>> all the days of my life,
and I will dwell in the house of the LORD
>> forever.

For Next Week

Read Acts 8:26–40 in preparation for next week's lesson.

Session 12

Philip Explains the Gospel to an Ethiopian

(Acts 8:26–40)

Focus

Theme: Window of Opportunity

Law/Gospel Focus

All people are separated from God because of sin. By nature, no one has a saving knowledge of God and His will. Yet Christ is the fulfillment of God's purpose and plan. Through faith in Jesus' death and resurrection, we know God's plan of salvation and are motivated by His love to seek windows of opportunity whereby we can tell others of His love for them.

Objectives

By the power of the Holy Spirit working through God's Word, we will
1. describe how God through faith enabled Philip to seize a window of opportunity to share God's plan of salvation revealed and fulfilled in the person and work of Jesus;
2. identify Holy Baptism as the means through which God brings people into a relationship with Him;
3. affirm the grace of God given to us at our Baptism;
4. seek windows of opportunity in which we can tell others of God's plan of salvation for all people.

Opening Worship

Read in unison Isaiah 53:7–8. Point out that these were the words read by the Ethiopian in the account we will study today.

He was oppressed and afflicted,
      yet He did not open His mouth;
He was led like a lamb to the slaughter,
      and as a sheep before her shearers is silent,
      so He did not open His mouth.
By oppression and judgment He was taken away.
      And who can speak of His descendants?
For He was cut off from the land of the living;
      for the transgression of my people He was stricken.

Introduction

1. What is the meaning of the expression "window of opportunity"?

2. Describe a situation in which you have heard or have spoken this expression.

3. How might "window of opportunity" be an apt expression to describe a situation in which you might have the chance to tell others of God's love for you in Christ Jesus? When might or have these "windows of opportunity" occurred?

In today's lesson, Philip seizes a "window of opportunity" provided to him by God to tell an Ethiopian of God's plan of salvation revealed and fulfilled in the person and work of Jesus.

Inform

Read Acts 8:26–40 and the commentary that follows.

About the Text

The Book of Acts is the second volume of the story of Jesus and the early church. (The Gospel of Luke is the first volume.) Acts portrays the faith and life of the apostles and the first converts to Christianity from the ascension of Jesus to Paul's house arrest in Rome. A central theme, of course, is mission—the growth of the church by the power and direction of the Holy Spirit. When Jesus gave the command to preach repentance and forgiveness in His name, He also promised the disciples "power from on high" (Luke 24:49). From the day of Pentecost onward, the church was engaged in a bold witness to the death and resurrection of Jesus—God's plan of salvation. "Let all Israel be assured of this," Peter proclaimed, "God has made this Jesus, whom you crucified, both Lord and Christ" (Acts 2:36).

While Peter, James, and John dominate the first part of Acts, and Paul the last section, Luke also includes brief episodes about the ministry of other prominent Christian leaders. The story of Philip, one of the seven deacons chosen to assist the 12 apostles, is set against the scattering of the believers after Stephen's death (7:59–60). As a faithful servant of Christ, Philip preaches the message in Samaria. Luke reports that "great joy" filled the disciples and crowds as a result of Philip's ministry (8:4–8). Though Philip on occasion met with difficulties, especially from Simon the magician, his efforts were richly blessed by the Lord.

Gaza was one of five Philistine settlements near the Mediterranean coast. Some 50 miles from Jerusalem, Gaza was the last village before the long desert road to Egypt. Philip's assignment, then, stretches the borders of the Christian mission. He is personally directed by an angel of the Lord, and begins his journey in the strength and grace of Jesus, his Lord and Savior.

The kingdom of Ethiopia existed as an independent state in Africa for thousands of years before Christ. The eunuch is an educated, influential man, with access to vast wealth and power in Queen Candace's court. (The title "Candace" was hereditary for all

Ethiopian queens.) Yet the eunuch is also a deeply spiritual man, perhaps a convert to Judaism (a "proselyte"). He believes in the true God and worships at the temple in Jerusalem. He is obviously committed to his faith, with a strong desire to learn more from God's will, to have made the long journey from his native country. The fact that he owns a scroll of Isaiah speaks volumes about his wealth and his commitment to hear and understand God's Word. (Books in the ancient world were hand-copied and thus very expensive.) At the same time, though, the eunuch is not eligible for full membership in the community. Because they had access to queens and to kings' harems, eunuchs were castrated; that is, their testicles were removed, often at a young age in anticipation of royal service. Such individuals were excluded from the assembly of Israel (Deuteronomy 23:1).

Philip first obeys the Spirit by staying near the chariot and then boldly inquires whether the Ethiopian understands the meaning of God's Word. Philip is sensitive to the situation and finds the perfect "window of opportunity" to present the Good News about Jesus.

The Ethiopian is reading Isaiah 53:7–8, most likely from an Aramaic or Greek translation of the Old Testament. The prophet's words reveal the heart of the Good News about Jesus: He is the Servant of God who suffers and dies for the sins of the world.

Philip's testimony undoubtedly included the following points: (a) Jesus was led to His death at the hands of the religious leaders and Roman authorities. He was the Suffering Servant, the innocent Lamb of God (John 1:29), who was silent before His enemies and judges. He was falsely accused and wrongly convicted. He was sentenced to die in a travesty of justice. (b) The Servant of the Lord in Isaiah's prophecy acts wisely and is exalted (52:13), is despised and rejected (53:3), takes our sorrow and sin upon Himself (53:4–5), and is punished and killed for the sake of His chosen people (e.g., 53:7, 10). Jesus is the Servant who fulfills in His passion, death, and resurrection all the Scripture passages about the Messiah. The fulfillment of the Scriptures is a key theme in Luke and Acts. (See Luke 24:25–26, 44–47; Acts 3:18.)

The eunuch's question demonstrates the centrality of Baptism in Christian preaching and teaching. Philip, like Peter on Pentecost, shares the Good News that God has chosen to make people full members of His kingdom through the washing of water and the Word. The Great Commission (Matthew 28:16–20), given by Jesus, directs the church to "make disciples" by baptizing and teaching the Good News to all nations. Philip first teaches, then baptizes, the Ethiopian.

Philip is taken away by the Spirit of the Lord. God the Spirit brings the mission to a conclusion, just as the angel (or messenger) opened the mission. The eunuch's response is joy—a fruit of the Spirit (Galatians 5:22) and the blessings of faith in Christ.

Luke notes God's blessings of guidance, strength, and protection as Philip is sent to a new "mission field." In truth, mission and ministry are never finished on earth; one conversion does not mean the end of work in the harvest fields. The work continues, day and night, in many different people and locations.

Discussing the Text

1. What is the central theme of the Book of Acts?

2. Describe the Ethiopian eunuch.

3. What "window of opportunity" does Philip seize?

4. What points were probably included in Philip's testimony to the Ethiopian?

5. How does the Ethiopian's question demonstrate the centrality of Baptism in the life of a Christian?

Connect

The story of Philip and the Ethiopian offers valuable insights for our Christian faith and life. (1) The Ethiopian understands the harsh truth of separation and spiritual ignorance. He is excluded from full membership in the religious community because of His condition. All people, however, are ultimately separated from God because of *sin*. The Ethiopian lacks a complete knowledge of God and His saving purpose. Again, by nature, no one has a saving knowledge of God and His will. The truth is unavoidable: on our own, we are unable to fear, love, and trust God as we should. Yet Christ is the fulfillment of God's purpose. By faith in Him—in His death and resurrection as God's solution to our dire need—we know God's plan of salvation. Jesus offered Himself, the perfect sacrifice, for the sins of the world. We are His chosen people, saved by His mercy and grace.

(2) The Ethiopian recognizes his *personal* need. As Philip proclaims the truth of God's judgment upon sin and call to repent, the eunuch, like the first converts at Pentecost, is "cut to the heart" (Acts 2:37). He believes God's Word. He feels his guilt. The Spirit is at work in his life. Philip's message, then, is the same as Peter's: "Repent and be baptized" (Acts 2:38). Baptism brings all people into a new relationship with the living God. Baptism is the "the washing of rebirth and renewal by the Holy Spirit" (Titus 3:5), God's appointed means to forgive sin and strengthen His people for service in the Kingdom. In our Baptism into Christ, we are connected with His crucifixion and resurrection (Romans 6:4). We share in His death, that we may also share in His life—now and forever.

1. What valuable insights does the account of Philip and the Ethiopian provide to you?

2. How is your Baptism a central focus of your Christian faith? How might it become more of a focus for you?

3. Consider "windows of opportunity" you may have to share God's good news of salvation through faith in Jesus Christ.

Vision

To Do This Week

Family Connection

1. Have a baptismal birthday party. Bring out pictures taken at the Baptism of each member of the family. Recall important events from that day. Make a birthday cake that says, "Baptized with Christ."

2. Discuss the term "window of opportunity." Discuss specific windows of opportunity each member of the family may have to share his or her faith in Jesus. Pray that the Holy Spirit would provide you these windows of opportunity and help you to identify them when they occur.

3. Read and discuss the Holy Baptism portion from Luther's Small Catechism. Have different members of the family illustrate the blessings, significance, and power of Holy Baptism.

Personal Reflection

1. Confess your sinful neglect to seize "windows of opportunity" to share your faith in Christ Jesus. Rejoice in the forgiveness Jesus merited for you on the cross. Pray that the Holy Spirit would empower you to boldly seize new "windows of opportunity" that you may encounter.

2. Praise God for that which He accomplished in your Baptism.

3. List "windows of opportunity" that you will look for this week to share your faith.

Closing Worship

Pray together the prayer for missionary work.

Almighty God, since You have called Your Church to witness that in Christ You have reconciled us to Yourself, grant that by Your Holy Spirit we may proclaim the good news of Your salvation that all who hear it may receive the gift of salvation; through Jesus Christ, our Lord. Amen.

For Next Week

Read Acts 9:1–20; 11:19–30 in preparation for next week's lesson.

Session 13

Early Christians Spread the Good News

(Acts 9:1–20; 11:19–30)

Focus

Theme: Dead Wrong!

Law/Gospel Focus

Because of their sinful nature, people seek to find hope and comfort, as well as a salve for their guilty consciences, in the created, rather than the Creator. God's Law shows us that any attempts on our own to save ourselves are dead wrong. God revealed in Christ His mercy and, by His Good News of Jesus' death on the cross for sinners, has brought us to repentance and faith, forgiving all of our sins. His great love for us in Christ gives us hope and comfort as we look forward to the new life we will enjoy with Him forever.

Objectives

By the power of the Holy Spirit working through God's Word, we will

1. explain how Saul was "dead wrong" in his zeal to squash the spread of Christianity;
2. describe the transformation that God worked in Saul as he was brought to faith;
3. identify ways in which people today are "dead wrong" as they seek to find hope, comfort, and meaning in life apart from Jesus Christ;
4. confess the hope and comfort God has provided to you through faith in Jesus.

Opening Worship

Sing together the following stanzas of "Jesus Shall Reign."

Jesus shall reign where'er the sun
Does its successive journeys run;
His kingdom stretch from shore to shore
Till moons shall wax and wane no more.

To Him shall endless prayer be made,
And praises throng to crown His head;
His name like sweet perfume shall rise
With ev'ry morning sacrifice.

People and realms of ev'ry tongue
Dwell on His love with sweetest song;
And infant voices shall proclaim
Their early blessings on His name.

Introduction

"You are 'dead wrong.' "

1. In what situation have you heard or spoken these words?

2. Although the phrase "dead wrong" may be used in many different contexts, what special meaning does it take on when referring to those who seek a relationship with God apart from Jesus Christ?

3. How might "dead wrong" be an apt description of a person who confesses the following:

"I try to be a good person. That's got to be worth something to God."

"There are many different ways to heaven."

"I need to try harder to please God."

In today's lesson, we see zealous Saul attempting to squash the spread of Christianity. He was dead wrong in his attempts to keep God's Law. But God, in His love for all people, transformed Saul—converting him—and uses him to boldly tell others of Jesus Christ, who willingly suffered and died on the cross for all people so no one would have to stand in judgment before God as "dead wrong."

Inform

Read Acts 9:1–20; 11:19–30; and the commentary that follows.

About the Text

"For I am the least of the apostles and do not even deserve to be called an apostle, because I persecuted the church of God. But by the grace of God I am what I am, and His grace to me was not without effect" (1 Corinthians 15:9–10).

Paul (Saul) was once a Pharisee, a strict adherent to the religious beliefs and values of his family and teachers. He was dutiful, loyal, and energetic. He was also, by his own admission, a fanatic—a murderer! The story of his change of heart, his conversion and call to ministry, is a tribute to the limitless mercy and grace of Jesus Christ, the world's only Redeemer.

The Book of Acts includes three separate accounts of Saul's conversion: (1) the actual event (9:1–31); (2) a summary report before the Jews in Jerusalem (22:1–21); and (3) a defense speech before the Roman procurator Festus and King Agrippa at Caesarea (26:1–32). In his own letters, Paul also describes his background, his role in persecuting the first apostles and disciples, and his dramatic "turn" to repentance and faith in the Lord Jesus (see Galatians 1:13–24; Philippians 3:2–11; 1 Timothy 1:12–17). Each part, like a piece of a puzzle, offers insights into the "life" and "new life" of the apostle to the Gentiles.

As a Pharisee, Saul was thoroughly trained in the Mosaic Law. His desire and personal mission were to study and obey the commandments of God, as well as to teach others to follow the covenant regulations. When Stephen and early Christians proclaimed that the Law was fulfilled in Jesus and that God accepts people by His grace in Christ, Saul was outraged. The core of his convictions was now threatened; the only recourse was direct confrontation—to destroy both the message and the messengers!

Saul was present at and approved of Stephen's stoning (Acts 8:1). Immediately afterward, he sought permission to arrest and imprison any and all followers of the new faith. His passion for crushing the movement took him far beyond the borders of Israel to the chief city of Syria—Damascus. A letter from the high priest (9:2) would open doors for Saul's mission and grant access to local synagogues. Since the decrees of the religious leaders were valid throughout the world, Saul was empowered by law to "extradite" Christians to stand trial in Jerusalem. Perhaps he was aware of strong resentment and hostility toward disciples in Damascus. Whatever the reason, though, Saul began his attack on the church with the long journey north, accompanied by trusted companions.

But the mission to Damascus takes an abrupt detour with the Lord's revelation to Saul. The "light from heaven" (9:3) may have been a blinding bolt of lightning or a supernatural ray of sunlight; the outcome, however, is the real focus of the story. Saul lies silently on the ground, broken and helpless. "Why do you persecute Me?" (v. 4) both demands an answer and identifies the heavenly voice. Jesus, the once-crucified but now risen Lord of the universe, speaks; He sees the hardships of His people—His body—and therefore acts to oppose the enemies of His church.

The risen Jesus directs Saul "into the city" (v. 5). Tarsus was a prosperous, prominent city in the southwest corner of Asia Minor (modern Turkey). Along with Athens (Greece) and Alexandria (Egypt), it was a major center of learning in the ancient world.

Saul's companions hear, but do not understand, the voice (see Acts 22:9). They stand dazed with their leader, their ambitions shattered by the mysterious revelation. Saul, once a powerful predator, is now completely humbled, blind, and unable and unwilling to eat and drink.

Ananias is a pious, faithful Jew. He is naturally reluctant to assume a major role in this extraordinary plan. Yet the Lord Jesus directs the mission of His church by His grace and strength. Saul is *His* "chosen instrument" (9:15). Saul's background, education, personality, and even his Roman citizenship are simply "tools" in the Master's hands. The Lord alone calls and saves sinful human beings. The Lord alone equips and sends forth His people to serve in the world. Saul is singled out and commissioned to preach and teach the Good News of forgiveness and salvation to Israel, but above all, to the Gentiles. As the Lord was hated, abused, and rejected, so too will Saul suffer for the Savior and His Word.

Ananias faithfully obeys the Lord and brings God's gifts of healing, forgiveness, a new calling, and the Holy Spirit, to Saul. The persecutor and murderer thus passes from darkness into light! He is baptized and filled with the Holy Spirit. Saul learns that through water and the Word, the Lord rescues His people from eternal condemnation. Jesus builds His kingdom through ordinary yet powerful means of His mercy and love. In grace, He brings Saul to faith and into fellowship with the saints.

The persecution of the Church in Jerusalem, though painful, did spark a mission beyond the Jewish nation and people. Some disciples, perhaps converted at Peter's Pentecost sermon, travel to Antioch and share the Good News with the Greeks—pure Gentiles (11:19–21). The capital of the Roman province of Syria, Antioch was a commercial center and later became "home" to the Gentile mission. St. Luke affirms God's providence and blessing: "The Lord's hand was with them," that is, with the missionaries (v. 21). Despite a rough beginning in Jerusalem, the ministry of the Word grows, as many people hear and believe the message of salvation.

Barnabas is originally from Cyprus but faithfully serves the Lord in the church at Jerusalem. His ministry to the believers in Antioch—at the request of the apostles—personifies his name: "Son of Encouragement" (Acts 4:36). In time, Barnabas shares the ministry at Antioch with Paul, and the church there grows in faith and membership. The pagan residents of the city likely attached the name "Christian" to the disciples, those who "belong to Christ." God's people are "little Christs," followers of Jesus' Word and ways.

Discussing the Text

1. Why does Paul refer to himself as the "least of the apostles and do not even deserve to be called an apostle" (1 Corinthians 15:9)?

2. How did Saul's mission to Damascus take an abrupt detour?

3. Why was Ananias reluctant to assume a major role in God's plan?

4. How did Jesus use Paul to build His church?

5. How might you describe Saul's life as "dead wrong" at first, then "alive right" in the end?

Connect

Consider how Paul's conversion and call apply to our life of faith today. (1) Paul is brutally honest in his writings. Though he thought he was doing God's will in persecuting the church, he soon learned he was wrong—dead wrong! Paul was fighting God. Paul was denying, even trying to destroy, God's plan for the salvation of the world. He was, by his own admission, the "worst of sinners" (1 Timothy 1:15). Yet Paul is no different from any other person: we are all sinners in the sight of God. The Law shows us our sinfulness and offers no hope to save us, to strengthen us, or to soothe our guilty consciences. Like Paul, though, we see God's mercy revealed in Christ. By His Word, Jesus has converted us—brought us to repentance and faith—and forgiven all our sins. He has called us by His Good News to new life and now empowers us to serve Him as Lord.

(2) Paul recognizes that God's judgment is global. No one, regardless of race or background or achievement, is excluded from the threat of condemnation. Because sin cuts across national boundaries and ethnic divisions, humankind needs full, universal salvation. Jesus is the world's *one* Redeemer. For Paul, no other name will be proclaimed to rulers and peoples throughout the Roman empire. All of Israel's hopes for redemption, all the yearnings of Gentiles for inclusion as God's holy people, are now found in Christ.

1. Describe how your life was "dead wrong" and is now "alive right."

2. Why is it appropriate that we, like Paul, echo the confession that we are "the worst of sinners"?

3. What does Paul's ministry tell us about the importance of inclusion—that Jesus Christ came to save all people?

Vision

To Do This Week

Family Connection

1. Act out the story of Saul's conversion. Then ask, "What did Saul do to deserve Jesus' forgiveness? What did we do to deserve Jesus' forgiveness?"

2. Discuss the phrase "dead wrong." Describe how, through Jesus, God has made us "alive right."

3. Discuss with family members people whom each would like to share Jesus' love. Pray together that the Holy Spirit would enable you to boldly tell of God's love for you in Christ Jesus with friends and loved ones.

Personal Reflection

1. Confess, "I am the worst of sinners!" Then rejoice in the forgiveness that Jesus merited for you on the cross.

2. Consider how God takes ordinary people, like you and me, and uses them to accomplish His purposes. How might He be using you now? How might He use you in the future?

3. Share the joy you have received through faith in Christ Jesus with someone this week.

Closing Worship

Sing or speak together the last two stanzas of "Jesus Shall Reign."

> Blessings abound where'er He reigns:
> The pris'ners leap to lose their chains,
> The weary find eternal rest,
> And all who suffer want are blest.
>
> Let ev'ry creature rise and bring
> Honor peculiar to our King;
> Angels descend with songs again,
> And earth repeat the loud amen.